John Nichol, Sydney Dobell

Thoughts on Art, Philosophy and Religion

selected from the unpublished papers of Sydney Dobell - With introductory note by

John Nichol

John Nichol, Sydney Dobell

Thoughts on Art, Philosophy and Religion
selected from the unpublished papers of Sydney Dobell - With introductory note by John Nichol

ISBN/EAN: 9783337234751

Printed in Europe, USA, Canada, Australia, Japan

Cover: Foto ©Thomas Meinert / pixelio.de

More available books at **www.hansebooks.com**

SELECTIONS FROM THE UNPUBLISHED PAPERS

OF

SYDNEY DOBELL.

Yrs heartily Sydney Dobell.

THOUGHTS

ON

ART, PHILOSOPHY, AND RELIGION:

SELECTED FROM THE UNPUBLISHED PAPERS

OF

SYDNEY DOBELL.

WITH INTRODUCTORY NOTE BY

JOHN NICHOL, M.A. Oxon., LL.D.

PROFESSOR OF ENGLISH LITERATURE IN THE
UNIVERSITY OF GLASGOW.

LONDON:
SMITH, ELDER, & CO., 15 WATERLOO PLACE.
1876.

[*All rights reserved.*]

INTRODUCTORY NOTE.

THE following pages, which—(with the exception of Letters and critical notes more properly belonging to a Biography)—contain all the unpublished Prose writings of Mr. Dobell likely to be of general interest, embrace two comparatively finished Essays and numerous suggestions or outlines for more elaborate treatment.

The Pamphlet on Parliamentary Reform—the only portion of this volume previously printed—was issued in 1865, and shortly afterwards reached a second edition. From this several paragraphs have been omitted, in some instances because a clearer statement of the same view appears to be found in the subjoined political notes, in others because they have seemed to be digressions detracting from the force of the argument. Considerable omissions are indicated by asterisks. The Editors have assumed the responsibility of a few minor changes, affecting the expression, never the sense of the author's view; the pressure under which the pamphlet was composed, with unfavourable conditions of health, having led, here and there, to an excessive involution of style.

The Lecture on Poetry addressed to the members of the Edinburgh Philosophical Institution (session 1856–57) is published as it was delivered, with no further change than has been involved in the insertion of a few quotations referred to. A large proportion of the notes which follow were marked as illustrative of the Lecture : others have been brought together from various manuscripts. These sections will be read with the interest attaching to a genuine artist's review of his own art. They convey with lucid and logical eloquence a clearly conceived theory, and are adorned by some of the most subtle passages—see especially the admirable analysis of Thorwaldsen's 'Night'—to be found in English criticism.

The Sketches from Nature, scattered among a multitude of note-books running over more than fifteen years and embracing almost every variety of subject, have been collected and reproduced, with rare omissions, as they were found. Several of these are mere fragments, gems of which a single facet has been cut, or half-finished cameos ; none it has appeared to us without some peculiar suggestiveness which justifies its insertion. Mr. Dobell was emphatically a poet of Nature, in whose sole society, outside his inner circle, perhaps too much of his life was spent. He physically saw more of the external world than other men, his eye had grown fine to her forms and tints, his ear to her voices. He had made himself, by study, a capable naturalist, and though looking on all things 'in the light that never was on sea or shore' his descriptions of plants, birds, the lustres on moor and hill, and the radiances of sun and cloud are conspicuously accurate. The incompleteness even of those sketches is not without its advantage; in recording first impressions his imagination is kept within limit, we escape the occasional excess of his detail. They have the charm of the first outlines for an artist's gallery.

The selection of the remaining—among them some of the most valuable—fragments has been a work of graver responsibility demanding a greater amount of discrimination. They have been gathered from a chaos of Memoranda,[1]—thrown together with no attempt at method and of various date—and arranged under heads

---

[1] I must disclaim any share in this work, beyond the *labor limæ* necessary for farther condensation, and testify to the unwearied industry and devoted zeal of my co-editor (Mr. Dobell's literary executrix), by which it has been accomplished.

as they have seemed to be naturally associated, *i.e.* to relate to the same class of subjects or train of thought. In cases where one idea reappears under several forms that held to be the maturest or best expression of the author's mind has been made to stand for the rest. It is hoped that, as a result of this process—which has eliminated about half the matter at our disposal—nothing is here presented which (allowing for the conditions of the composition) will do injustice to the writer, or be without some claim on the reader's attention.

The concluding section of this volume has a special interest as containing the results of many years' inevitably intermittent thought on the continuation of the work which—in spite of manifest incongruities—must be regarded as Mr. Dobell's masterpiece. One of its radical defects, an utter want of unity, unfortunately appears in the conception of what remains to represent this continuation. The first impression will be one of disappointment. We come to hear the Play, and are put off with a performance before the curtain : we want to learn how the essence of egotism whom we know as Balder is to be humanised, and we find him hidden. It is evident that the poet had been constrained to postpone the execution of his portentous plan. The Epic Drama of Life

—for a mere interlude in which these notes were, in the first instance, intended as a mere outline—was cast on a scale too colossal for execution. The torso left attests in scope and detail the vast compass of the author's mind and his lack of the sense of proportion. He never seems to have heard of the Statute of limitations imposed on all who desire to leave a definite and abiding mark on an age so manifold as ours, and he aspired in the nineteenth to the universal views of the seventeenth century.

The dramatic sketch in the following pages is given as nearly as possible in the words of the memoranda. It has been thought desirable in some instances considerably to condense the original; the headings of scenes which must have owed their interest to expression in a completed form have been occasionally omitted, together with passages of prose and verse too fragmentary to stand by themselves; but the substance of all that is essential to the plot, the delineations of the chief actors, and all details that appear at once intelligible and interesting have been preserved.

The scene of the Play [1] is laid in some undetermined

---

[1] Mr. Dobell had abandoned the idea of making it an Interlude, and, had time and strength permitted, would have wrought it out as a separate and substantive Drama.

locality, toward the close of the first half of the fifteenth century, *i.e.* the period of the general councils, the Hussite War, the last of the Antipopes of Avignon, and the beginnings of that Art which was destined to strike a deadlier blow against an irresponsible Priesthood than had been possible to the great German Emperors. The strife—perhaps the most momentous in modern history—of the House of Hohenstaufen with the Church of Hildebrand was about to be renewed under changed conditions. The poet had it in his mind to celebrate one of the later phases of the war of Guelf and Ghibelline, and that he did not approach his task without adequate preparation the copious historical, biographical, antiquarian and literary references in his common-place book abundantly attest. He had studied the leading characters, the prevalent superstitions—the Alchemy, Astrology, and Demonology—all the salient manners and customs of the age, and made himself master of the issues at stake with an amount of research and judgment which might have qualified him to write a great historic poem. That he would ultimately have more closely associated his imaginary with real events and persons is probable. To the Plot, as it exists in germ, there attaches a degree of ideal vagueness. The unnamed city on the plain, the knight's castle on the hill, the loves of Heretica and the Cardinal, and the disguise of the Secretary are like elements of an ecclesiastical Faery Tale. But, under the masks of representative men and situations, we are presented with a substantially accurate and vivid picture of the conflicting passions, principles and interests of the age. The poet's love of liberty on the one hand, his deep religious sympathies on the other, vetoing an absolute adhesion to either party in the struggle, enable him to pronounce on each in turn an impartial verdict. The Cardinal—until his whole nature is dismantled by the catastrophe—is a noble type of a good Priest—a brave champion of what is best in the old order of things. The Chancellor—(as seems to us the author's most dramatic conception) is a corrupt and scheming statesman. But we are made to realize that the latter is on the side of the Future. Of the other 'dramatis personæ' few are sufficiently developed to afford much scope for criticism. Grand or striking thoughts are hung upon their lips : they are hardly, as yet, articulated into relationship or set in motion. The Duchess is a shadowy Cleopatra ; Heretica a ray of white light ; the Abbot a zealot, made the vehicle for numerous parodies (one of which it has been thought sufficient to present) of mediæval pedantry and fanaticism culminating in frenzy. The Philosopher is the spokesman of the early science which, previously represented only by Roger Bacon, the Alchemists, the Arabians, and at the half eastern court of Frederick II., was about to have a new dawn in Germany and Florence. Embodying 'the spirit of the years to come,' we may imagine (as indeed appears from the Memoranda), that he would have been made the mouth-piece of much of the author's own Philosophy. Of that philosophy some indications are given in the extracts under the three headings of the present volume which precede the Play. In pronouncing on these the reader will constantly revert to the manner in which they were written, and the form in which they have been found : but, with all deductions, it is believed they will be received by more than the poet's personal friends as acceptable memorials of a singularly comprehensive mind, unweariedly active in the search after Beauty and Truth,—qualities which he identified in the meeting point of a Religious Ideal, and with which, in the spirit of a philanthropy to which the merely sensuous school of Art is a stranger, he desired to permeate the world of his influence.

No compact system of thought is to be looked for in

these pages. Like Coleridge's 'Aids to Reflection,' or his 'Confessions,' they set forth the imperfectly formularized sometimes imperfectly consistent conclusions of an enquiring spirit. Nor is the manner in which they are expressed invariably faultless. Books are written to be read, or to be reviewed, or because their ideas have come to the writer, like the numbers to a poet. To the last category the bulk of our author's prose belongs: and to it adhere the advantages and drawbacks of such a manner of composition. More of a thinker than an orator, he seldom had his audience in view: but if criticism failed to prune his exuberance, neither did he suffer from its torpedo torch. He may claim place with those

> 'Children of the second Birth
> Whom the world could not tame,'

spoken of by Mr. Arnold in his verses on 'Obermann.'

The range of Mr. Dobell's general reading was limited; he preferred to wander in comparatively pathless fields: he fell in love with strange conceptions, and had a weakness for coining curious words; his book learning was quaint and peculiar. Hence it not unfrequently occurs that he unconsciously reproduces results more or less familiar to students of the ancient and modern classics; he constructs what has been long ago constructed, and slays the slain. But he arrives at his conclusions in an original manner by processes demonstrably his own. His speculations have thus a special interest, as showing how much a powerful mind can achieve without the modern Historical method, which when exclusively employed is apt to rob our thought of freshness and vitality. He often conveys to us the impression of a man transplanted from that old age which is the youth of the world restoring our jaded senses with legends of the prime. Mr. Dobell's style is unequal: admirably clear and forcible at its best, it is occasionally the involved record of super-subtle dialectic, overlaid with thick coming fancies and defaced by Latinisms. Of the Pedantry which consists in the desire to dignify platitudes by old-fashioned dress he had no share, but he is at intervals led astray by an anatomical Philology, or a Nominalism like that of Plato's Cratylus. In argument he never knows when to have done. His composition is apt to resemble that of the Chinese puzzles where one elaborate ivory box is carved inside of another. His illustrations are excellent, but the illustrations of the illustrations are confusing. His mental analysis often reminds us of the reported exordium of one of Fichte's lectures 'Think the wall: think the thinker of the wall :—think the mind that thought the thinker of the wall.'

When travelling in those regions where Truth as well as Error resides in a maze he does not always succeed in finding the clue, or at all events in leading others through the labyrinth. In the purely speculative fragments, some of which have been gathered from MS. headed notes for a work on the Physiology of Nations, he mixes physics and metaphysics in a fashion for which we may find parallels in Browne or Burton,—in the otherwise opposite schools of Descartes and of Hartley. In one passage he adopts without knowing its source or realizing its consequences, the view of the Will which identifies it with Desire: in another he elevates it into an independent and main factor of life, and propounds theories of the origin of Knowledge which recall those of the German Idealists. His abstract thoughts are those of a man talking to himself and refuting objectors in an inner Socratic dialogue. ὁ μὲν ἐντὸς διάλογος ἄνευ φωνῆς γενόμενος. But even his fantasies are instructive; however abrupt or startling, his conclusions are invariably genuine and often luminous. Academic witlings whose being is a grin *et præterea nihil* may isolate passages of his writing and subject them to the ridicule which they conceive to be the test of Truth; but when read with their context they will be found to form part of an intelligible though scarce fulfilled design, and, though sometimes beneath crude forms, to teem with the wisdom which justifies itself. The poet's expression is vivid and his judgment sound on all that his eye sees or his soul feels; he fails when he becomes technical or leans upon erudition.

The connecting link and concentrating aim of his Philosophy is the search after an Ideal which he finds realized in the Perfect Man—according to his belief the only practical standard for the Race—of primitive Christianity, and so rises or passes from Theory to Faith. His views on this head are partially developed in the Religious Fragments which will probably be to many readers the most interesting in the volume.

For various reasons it is impossible here to supplement what is wanting to the exposition of a Creed which, even in some of its essentials, Mr. Dobell himself hesitated to formularize. A more truly religious man never lived, every action and thought of his life was pervaded by the spirit of reverence—but he adhered to no sect, and no form of so-called orthodoxy could claim his allegiance. He was equally antagonistic to what he conceived to be the enervating ecclesiasticism of Rome and to the Juggernaut worship which is most consistently expounded in Calvinism. But he dwelt more on the affirmative than on the negative side of his belief, and was as averse to dogmatic denial as to blind credulity. Attaching himself to a liberal but careful interpretation of Gospel History, his sympathies probably lay more with the broadest section of the broad Church of England than with any other recognized denomination.

Our author's Politics, as his Theology, were marked by that absolute independence which in Art would accept no copies but Nature, in life no guides but Duty and the Graces. The views in the Reform Pamphlet are in general accord with those of Mr. Mill (with which it may be remarked he was unfamiliar), but they are obviously developed from the writer's mind. They are infected with his prejudices—(*e.g.* his extreme intolerance of American institutions, his comparative ignorance of the Teutonic, his love of the Latin races, only restrained by his equal abhorrence of the Cloister and the Commune between which those races oscillate)—and by the historical incompleteness of a view which in contrasting Republics and Hereditary Monarchy forgets the record of Athens on the one side and that of later Spain on the other.

But they are inspired by exhilarating aspirations and often marked by shrewd common sense.

At a time when the desire for literary completeness is justly stimulated by daily accumulating masses of incompetence, it may be objected that in the publication of these fragments we are bringing unripe fruit into a glutted market. Our hope is rather to have offered a handful of good seed that, scattered in various soils, may spring to various richness of bloom. We trust, at all events, to have enabled the reader to judge for himself regarding some leading features of a notable figure in the recent history of English thought.

J. N.

CONTENTS.

	PAGE
INTRODUCTORY NOTE	v

ARTISTIC.

LECTURE ON THE 'NATURE OF POETRY'	3
ILLUSTRATIVE NOTES ON POETRY AND ART	66
SKETCHES FROM NATURE	76

SPECULATIVE.

SEARCH FOR THE IDEAL	96
RELATION OF IMPERFECT TO IDEAL ACTION AND EXPRESSION	107
BEAUTY, LOVE, ORDER, UNITY	113
ORIGIN OF RHYTHM, SLEEP, &c.	128
NOTES ON LANGUAGE AND THOUGHT	135

RELIGIOUS.

THEORETIC	147
ETHICAL	181

POLITICAL.

PAMPHLET ON REFORM	197
SOCIAL NOTES	233

MEMORANDA AND FRAGMENTS OF PROJECTED PLAY.

PLAN AND DESIGN	255
MEMORANDA AND FRAGMENTS CONCERNING CHARACTERS	287
MISCELLANEOUS MEMORANDA FOR THE DRAMA	335

ARTISTIC

LECTURE ON THE 'NATURE OF POETRY.'

DELIVERED IN THE QUEEN STREET HALL, EDINBURGH, APRIL 8, 1857.

THE temper in which we perceive a fact to be accounted for is very different from that in which we construct a theory to explain it.

Looking at this Book, for instance, I may assert with some confidence that I see such and such a shape and colour; but I should speak in a different tone if I had to treat of the cause of colour or to answer the old vexed questions of form and substance. So I may have the greatest certainty that such and such works of a great Poet are Poems; but those of you who have the deepest intimacy with those works, and have gone nearest to the hidden qualities which make them what they are, will understand most thoroughly in how different a mood I shall enter this evening upon an enquiry as to the Nature of Poetry.

I would meet on the threshold of the subject some

objections that may arise in the course of what I have to say. Those of you who are already well exercised in such enquiries may perhaps complain that I have not compressed into my space as much detail as it might have held, and that throughout I have not dealt so much with the metaphysics of the question as was due to my audience.

I would answer to the first objection that as this is not an essay but a lecture, some repetitions may occasionally be necessary to keep up an easy continuity of Thought; and to the second that I have intentionally avoided what is commonly called metaphysics because as I have to-night, as far as regards the mind, to do more with phenomena than essences—with the *quomodo* than the *cur sit*—I wish to keep my subject as clear as possible from all unnecessary controversies.

As Poetry is a product of mental functions I have to deal with those functions; but I am concerned rather with the science of their activity, on which we can all agree, than with the philosophy of it, on which each of us should probably differ. I have therefore carefully abstained from the use of such words as—implying more than is needful for my purpose—raise unnecessary questions in the hearer, questions of the highest interest in themselves, but not vital to what we are about to consider.

Lastly, and most emphatically, I would ask of you all that if in some portions of my remarks I appear to claim more for the character of the Poet than Biography will justify, you will be good enough to suspend your judgments till you arrive at that part of my theory in which I endeavour to reconcile the Poet in the exercise of his vocation with the same Man—often as we know a very erring miserable man—under the ordinary circumstances of Life. With this brief preface I proceed at once to examine the Nature of Poetry.

In one of the books attributed to Aristotle we are told that artists should follow Zeuxis. You may remember that this great artist having promised to paint the Greeks an Helen, demanded to study from all the most beautiful women in Greece; and choosing from each the beauty wherein she excelled, combined their charms into a total perfection more beautiful than any. This consummate whole would be thenceforth the standard of female form; as a woman was more or less beautiful she would more or less resemble this incarnate Beauty, and for every portion of a female figure there would be one infallible criterion. If it could congruously make part of this perfect whole, it must be held perfect; and if it would be incongruous with that faultless shape, it must be considered in the same degree failing of perfection.

This gives us a tolerable notion of the judgment by ideals—so called of course not because the standard cannot really exist, but because this real perfection if truly built up of separately perfect parts may be supposed to agree as a whole with what Plato has called *the idea*— or that immaterial model in the Divine Mind after which each of God's works is created.

It is only by this judgment from ideals that we can, in anything, judge at once largely and accurately. In every reality there are, because it is imperfect, things which are not accounted for by its own individual instance, things inadequate and superadequate, questions without answers, and answers without questions. It is only in the Ideal Model that Perfection justifies itself, and the insoluble problems of each imperfect copy of it uncoil and join in beautiful and harmonious solution. It is only by attaining a just idea of the perfect Man that we can understand the World-old conflict concerning such questions as 'what is Truth,' 'what is Goodness,' 'what is Beauty.' It is only by associating such ideal *men* into the ideal of human society that one can graduate all the opposing theories of morality and politics, and see all their wrongs and contradictions conterminating in a central Right and Truth.

Nay, it is only by recognising this unattained *ideal*, and

the distance from it of our highest *real*, that we understand the ethical office of Religion and demonstrate the moral necessity of Revelation itself. My answer, therefore, to our question of to-night ' what is Poetry? ' is this : Poetry is whatever can congruously form part of a Poem : Perfect Poetry is whatever can congruously form part of a Perfect Poem. Our real business is therefore to enquire 'What is a Perfect Poem?'

Now since, for obvious reasons, we cannot *literally* imitate Zeuxis and combine the perfect portions of imperfect Poems into something from which we might deduce the laws of a perfect whole, we must carry the enquiry a step further back. I shall do so by laying down a postulate which I shall ask you to take awhile for granted, and I shall then, in the first part of this lecture, work out an hypothesis from this premiss : and in the second part of the lecture I shall adduce examples of existing poetry, and proceed to justify my hypothesis by showing that it explains the phenomena and is not inconsistent with established truths. In reply then to the question what is a Perfect Poem I answer *a perfect Poem is the perfect expression of a Perfect Human Mind.* Not only an expression, but a perfect expression, of not only a Mind, but a human Mind, and not only a human Mind, but a perfect human Mind. To show, by careful generalizations from the facts of History and Biography, the true character of a perfect human Mind, would in itself be a task not for one lecture but a series of lectures; and I shall therefore content myself to-night with an authority which, while higher than any human induction, is, as I need not tell such an audience as this—the very short-hand and brief of all Philosophies, and assume that 'in the Image of God made He man.' To discover the characteristic features of the Image we must therefore enquire the Attributes of the Original.

Now the manifestations by which the Supreme is best known to us are those of to Know, to Love, and to Make. And since a human mind can have no notion of the creation of Something out of Nothing, to Make, so far as we are concerned, must be understood as to Order. Order being that collocation of things which to the Divine Mind seems fit: and which we humanly express when we say that Order is a certain position of things with regard to each other regulated by the nature of the things: which state of position we call relation because each of the posited things refers the mind to the other.

An ideal Man, therefore, must by virtue of his Imageship be a Knower, a Lover, and a Maker. But since he is Image and not Original, created and not Creator, he must be something besides.

There must be that in him which expresses the relation of the thing made to the Maker.

Now that which in the less recognizes the greater, in the vassal acknowledges the Suzerain, the Saxons termed *Worthschipe*, from *Worth*, the residence of a Manorial Lord. Hence (and I must beg you to bear in mind the wide interpretation of the words) our verb 'to Worship.' The Ideal Man must, then, be a Worshipper.

The primary attributes of a perfect human Mind are, therefore, to Know, to Love, to Worship and to Order.

'To Know,' implies things that can be known. Existing in midst of those things, the ideal mind is roused to activity by them with the following results.

The things which it knows are true. The things which it loves are Beautiful. The things which it worships are sublime. The things which it 'makes' are ordered : order being that position of things regarding each other with which an ideal mind is pleased.

The ideal mind identifies Beauty and Sublimity as the magnetic needle identifies the North. The North is not the North because the needle points to it : but meanwhile it is sufficient for us to know that we can depend upon the needle.

The ideal mind receives Truth as a perfect eye

receives form and colour. What relation form and colour bear to the Absolute we cannot tell : it is sufficient that they are Truths to Beings organized as we are.

The ideal mind weaves order as a loom weaves a fabric. There is a higher reason why the fabric is what it is than the mechanism of the loom ; yet that lower reason is sufficient for practical purposes—and would perhaps be more useful than the higher if—as in the case of Man explaining Man—one loom had to account for the products of the other. And here let us again notice the importance of dealing with ideals when we arrive at the large simplicities of Nature. There can be no doubt that Love is the test of the Beautiful ; but if I had said the Beautiful is what a human being loves, a thousand facts would rise to contradict me. But though many minds love what is not beautiful, we all must notice that in proportion as a mind is high in the scale of humanity the objects of its Love are certain to graduate towards Beauty.

There can be no doubt that Worship is the test of the Sublime, though some nations bow down before the horrible and the ugly. But these fetish-worshippers are known to be, in every sense. the lowest form of humanity ; and in those nations where the human Nature is in other respects more highly developed we find the objects of reverence more and more sublime.

There can be no doubt that to make, in the sense of to order, is a power common to the human mind, though the result of its feebler exercise be too often but a complicated confusion—'non bene junctarum discordia semina rerum.' But as we rise to stronger characters we find them reducing those 'discordia semina' to a partial order or a forced consistency, resulting in systems each complete in itself, even though perhaps mutually irreconcilable. And as we still rise to yet higher minds we find a more and more general harmony and cosmos of thought, because both a clearer perception of separate things as they are and a correcter power of distributing them according to relations.

Thus ascending through the various grades of the real, and perceiving how at every step certain Laws have a wider and directer efficacy, we learn that to understand the full and true operation of those Laws (whose impeded and uncertain results in this our imperfect state perplex and puzzle us) we must rise still higher in the same direction, and look to that perfect type of the Ideal in which alone their action is general, simple, congruous, and infallible. Arriving there we find Love consecrated to the Beautiful, Worship intuitively loyal to the Sublime, Knowledge accepting only the True, and Order spontaneously co-ordinating the Related.

Here let no one found an objection on the ground of that Christian Charity which we owe to all Men, for on closer examination he will perceive that the true exercise of that universal Love depends on the very principle I have laid down. He who detects those elements of Beauty which exist beneath the ugliness of every sinner is exercising one of the most ennobling privileges of Christianity: but he who loves the faults even of his dearest friend is destroying, by that amiable vice, one of the Divinest safeguards of his own virtue. And let no man take exception to what I have said of Worship from any fear that it infringes on the first Commandment. In the first place I beg such an objector to notice that large significance of the term which I have pointed out when mentioning its derivations; and in the second place it would be easy to show, by applying certain Laws which I shall presently have to indicate, that those material things which we call sublime are but the visible expressions of the Invisible, and that when by the impulse of his reverence the Poet instinctively recognizes the Sublimities of this Universe, he is really but repeating in his own appointed fashion the great saying 'All Worship be to God alone.'

A perfect mind, then, possesses, in due proportion, every human quality, and is especially characterized by the powers to love, to worship, to know, and to order. And a perfect Poem is the perfect expression of such a mind.

To express is to carry out. To express a mind is to carry out that mind into some equivalent. And here I must beg you to observe carefully the sense in which I shall have to use this term 'equivalent,' because, as will be shown by-and-bye, the peculiar meaning attached to it is important to the whole theory. By an 'equivalent' I mean that product of an active mind, which being presented to the same mind when passive, would restore the former state of activity. I say not which being presented to another mind, but 'which being presented to the same mind.' For instance, the full verbal expression of a feeling of mine would be such words as if I heard them in a tranquil mind would excite that feeling into the same state of activity.

There is no essential difference in the forms of Poetic expression, but they may be conveniently divided, for our present purpose, into simple and compound.

Simple, as when the state of mind in the Expressor is directly succeeded by some external act, as of speech. As if, feeling Love, I should say, 'I love.' Compound, as when the mental activity is directly succeeded by *such facts of the imagination* as are its *equivalents*, which facts it has to express by such other equivalents as being equivalent to them are thus indirectly equivalent to itself. As if I should express the feeling of Love not by saying 'I love,' but by calling up in the imagination some beautiful object which is the equivalent of Love—that is, which would rouse my Love into activity—and finding for that object some equivalent in words—that is, such words as when the object has disappeared from my inward sight would make it reappear.

A compound or indirect expression is therefore a succession of direct expressions, and is, of course, more or less compound according to the number in the series between the original mental activity and the final external act, as of speech, for instance, which is its ultimate outcome. For example, in the illustration I have just given of the indirect expression of Love, the feeling finds its equivalent in the image of something beautiful, and this image finds its equivalent in words. This is the simplest form of compound. But, as we shall see by-and-bye, it may happen that there are no *verbal* equivalents for that 'something beautiful' which is the equivalent of the feeling, and that the 'something' must itself be expressed by another and equivalent beautiful image for which there happen to be adequate words. This, which I hope to illustrate presently, is the next form of compound.

In either case the verbal signs, the words, are the indirect expression of Love ; and the compound act will be perfect in proportion to the perfection of each of the simple acts whereof it is composed. It will be seen at a glance that no full utterance of a total human mind is likely to be wholly simple or wholly compound ; but as the one or the other predominates, the character of the total expression will be direct or indirect.

In a perfect Poem, therefore, the perfect mind may be said either to utter itself directly in a *truthful and orderly expression of Love and Worship*, or indirectly in a *loving and worshipful expression of ordered Truth*. The first may be called Lyrical, the second Epical Poetry ; though, as the peculiar forms of each became occasionally adopted for the other, the popular use of these names has lost sight of the original and essential distinctions. I do not mention the Drama among the great separate forms of Poetry, because the Drama is merely an Epic produced under compulsory external conditions that interfere with the natural laws of epical production. Much that I should wish to say on this most interesting of hybrids I am compelled by time and space to omit from the present enquiry.

The two great forms of Poetic expression, then,—the Epical and Lyrical—are governed by the same laws, and we will proceed therefore to investigate the one which, more or less, contains the other, and to enquire into the conditions of a Perfect Epic. We have seen that it is a perfect expression of a perfect human mind,—that is, something which being brought into contact with a perfect mind would rouse into action its characteristic and other qualities in due proportion ; and that it is an *indirect* expression—that is, such an equivalent as is not a simple utterance.

We have first, therefore, to find an equivalent not in words but in things for a mind possessing many faculties, of which what are popularly called the feelings are represented by to love and to worship, and the other functions by to know and to order. The problem is not to find an equivalent for either of these functions separately, but to produce a total that shall answer to them all. The faculty to know might perhaps find its equivalent in a chaos of Truths : the faculty to order in an arrangement of them : but to love and to worship exact that those Truths shall be either beautiful or sublime.

But we seek something more than even an orderly arrangement of things true, beautiful, and sublime : for the mind that has to find an equivalent is stated in the premiss to be not only a mind but a human mind. To those conditions, therefore, that are imposed by the faculties in which it is the *Image of God* we must add the conditions by which it is specially *marked and limited as Man.* And, since it is looking for an equivalent to itself among things other than itself, one primary condition of expression by such an equivalent must be the laws by which the human mind perceives—or the laws of what, to avoid metaphysical disquisitions, I will call the *inward eye.* And this familiar term is no mere figure of speech, for the body is so much the Poem and homologue of the soul that the laws of the inward eye may be illustrated by those of the outward. The outer eye has to do with the universe of external things; the inner eye has to do with that inner universe of facts which memory has stored and perception supplies, and with such new combinations of these as may take place under the direction of the other functions of the mind.

Now the great law of outward sight is that we perceive but one thing at a time. A combination of things is perceived by rapid discursions of the eye from the object which it principally regards to the surrounding objects, which become accessories to the object of principal attention and are united with it by an act of optical memory. The mental vision obeys the same law. The Truth on which the inward eye is chiefly fixed becomes a solar centre and other truths are apprehended by rapid excursions from this central point—to which they become, therefore, accessories ; each accessory (in proportion to the attention paid to it) itself the centre of still subordinate excursions. And as the bodily eye in perceiving a cluster of objects will do so more felicitously and perfectly if the object on which it chiefly rests be one of such size and position as to be a favourable centre for excursion, and of such general character as shall not conflict with the impressions of the others, so the mental eye for the perfect exercise of its powers needs that its principal Truths shall be central and generic, and by the—as it were mechanical—conditions of its functions requires for its happiest exercise to move under the direction of order.

Let us notice, for instance, the mode of the outer eye in dealing with facts which the Divine order has already regulated—an organized being. It strikes upon the most important portion, and by rapid unconscious excursions to the subordinate parts brings them into optical relation with the central fact : and in these unconscious excursions, however rapid, the same law prevails, and the members are perceived as wholes with regard to their parts by the same process whereby the total being is perceived as a whole with regard to its members. And it is because in an organized being *the Divine order has arranged* the facts of which it is composed that the eye can more rapidly get a true perception of such a being than of a chaotic mass of the same number of constituents. So with the eye of the mind. It fixes on some fact among the multitude of inner existences—some natural centre of many relations—and relates all referable facts to it by rapid unconscious excursions. In the same manner these subordinate facts are themselves made centres for their own appropriate relations, and the process extends downwards as far as perception goes. The mind is naturally disposed, therefore, to perceive a whole—something made up by the reference of many things to some one principal thing—and the perception will be felicitous and perfect (that is, the mind will use its natural functions with ease and advantage) in proportion as that great Whole and all its constituents are *ordered*.

I might have reached the same conclusions by a scrupulous analysis of our *notion* of 'order;' but as it would demand a closer consequence of thought than the present method, I shall content myself this evening with this argument—and it seems to me a sufficient argument—from analogy.

The hypothesis that a perfect Poem is the expression of a perfect Human Mind conducts us therefore to these primary laws for the construction of an Epic: that it must be an ordinated thing : that as to this arrangement it must be that of one subject with that subject's congruous accessories : and that such subject and accessories must be of a nature to satisfy Love (and its modifications) Worship and Knowledge ; must be generically True and specifically Beautiful and Sublime. And that the foregoing laws apply not only to the principal subject and its accessories, but to every part of which that whole is made up ; *i.e.* that the Great Poem is an organized aggregation of small Poems ; with this difference, that whereas the *sine quâ non* of the principal Truth in the Poem is its sublimity or beauty the *sine quâ non* of the principal Truth in the passage is its relationship, near or remote, to the central truth of the Greater Whole.

To which central truth it is related either directly, as in the cardinal portions, or as in the subordinate members—by virtue of its relationship to some other Truth still more nearly related than itself.

But we have said that a Perfect Epic is the perfect *expression* of a perfect human mind : and though we have now reached some notion of the *equivalent* of such a mind, we have not reached that of its expression because an expression is a given species of equivalent——an equivalent and something more. To express is, as we saw, to carry *out*. An expression therefore is an equivalent that can exist *out* of the mind. We have gone so far on our journey outward as to realize for the active faculties of the mind an equivalent in the facts of the imagination; let us take the last stage which crosses the boundaries of the inner and outer worlds and examine the vehicle in which this final carrying out is to take place. The mind may be 'carried out' more or less perfectly by bodily movement, by the inflexion and combination of inarticulate sounds, by the design of visible shapes and by the utterance of words. Hence we have Action, Music, Painting, Sculpture, Architecture, and Poetry. Of these methods our subject confines us to the last. It will be perceived that practically that 'last' contains all the others, since the Poet by means of words can evoke those others in the imagination of his hearer and really therefore express himself by all the arts at once: but we are now to consider the physical and external means by which he obtains possession of these and all other modes of expression, and must examine the conditions of *Poetic human Speech*. Those conditions must be, of course, the laws which govern the medium through which sound is produced, the organs by which we produce it, and the mind to which things are to be conveyed by means of it. As to the first, we know that sound is the result of undulations of air, and that to the shape of those undulations it is necessary there should be no collision between them. We find therefore *succession* to be a first condition of verbal sounds, we know that the same condition is that of the organs of utterance, and, as we have already noticed that law of the mind by which it perceives perfectly but one thing at a time, we know that succession is also the condition of perfect mental reception. But succession is the general condition of *all* verbal utterance, and we are now enquiring concerning a specific form of it—Poetic utterance—and shall expect therefore to discover some specific form of that general condition which shall produce perfect, as distinct from imperfect, utterance. It would be easy to show, and I will by-and-bye proceed to show, that the necessary conditions of such perfect utterance could be deduced from those higher data of the mind from which we have drawn the principles of the Poem to be uttered : but because I wish to demonstrate the thorough humanity of Poetry—that it not only answers to our Divinest faculties but is actually in tune with our material flesh and blood, we will again, if you please, turn to the laws of that body by which the mind receives and conveys sensation. I need only refer you to the science of acoustics to recall the well-known fact that the difference between a mere noise—or an imperfect and indistinct auditory sensation—and musical sounds—or a perfect and distinct sensation—depends on the degree to which the vibrations of air obey the laws of oscillation and interference ; those laws that result in *undulation* and provide that in a perfect sound the vibrations must recur after regular intervals of time. Whether in one of the original vibrations that make up the note,—where the interval may be but the 24,000th part of a second—or in the notes themselves,—between which the intervals are so much longer—the law is the same that the succession must have definite relations to a certain beaten time. (I need only refer you to the science of Harmony for illustrations of this familiar position.)

Now a succession of such a kind is a *rhythmic* succession. And since such a succession is the most perfect manner of propagating sound *through* air, and receiving it *from* air, it must also be the most perfect manner of communicating it *to* air. And since our organs are all constituted with special aptitude for their peculiar tasks, a rhythmic succession must be what it is *best for the mouth to produce and the ear to receive.*

Nay I think we might go further : for remembering those beautiful experiments by which Chladni,[1] Savart,

---

[1] The reader may perhaps remember, among the discoveries relating to phonics made by Chladni or Chladenius, the curious result of one of his experiments on plates of glass or metal - that a sonorous plate, fixed horizontally, having its upper surface regularly

and Wheatstone have shown to what a wonderful extent vibrations are propagated through matter, and when once set in motion are repeated by sympathetic and other action in innumerable reflexes, each bearing computable relations to the original impulse; remembering, too, that the laws of oscillation and interference are so wide as to extend from Chladni's grains of sand to Sun, Moon, and stars, and remembering that the two great sources of bodily sensation—sound and light—are already shown to be results of undulations that obey these laws, we shall be prepared, I think, to expect in the human body a *general* submission to principles to which it shows itself amenable in the external organs of hearing and seeing.

And turning to that body what do we find to confirm that expectation?

One of the most notable and well-known facts regarding that body is that its vitality depends upon the motion of an organ, the heart, whose motion is, in health, peculiar for its most accurate proportions. The interval of time between every healthy heart-throb is precisely equal to that of the throb itself. Physiology has already shown that other recognisable organic motions of the body—for instance, the action of the lungs—bear definite

strewed with sand, on being struck at the edge with a violin bow, not only gave a peculiar sound, but also exhibited a corresponding arrangement of the sand.—ED.

relations to this motion of the heart; and in all modesty I would suggest to the great Physiologists here present whether there be not reason to infer that every portion of the incessant vital action of the system is keeping measured dance to that great *beater of time*? If so it follows that any thoroughly congruous and felicitous outcome of functions so proportional in their action must be itself proportional, and that in so far as anything which those functions are called on to take up and convey is proportional it will be easily and harmoniously accepted. Perfect utterance, therefore, whether as a thing to be performed or as a thing to be received by those functions, must occur in a succession bearing proportional relations to a time marked by a series of equal intervals, that is, to the time beaten by a healthy heart.

Now rhythm, or musical time, is, as we all know, a succession of this nature, and we arrive therefore at the second condition of poetic utterance, that it shall be a *rhythmic succession*. And thus from the lower data— those of the body—we have reached the same condition for the physical utterance which from the higher data— of the mind—we have before deduced as one of the primary conditions of the ideal Poem to be uttered— *Proportion*. And by applying to this proportioned succession of *utterance* those same conditions concerning

Truth, Beauty, Sublimity, and Relationship, which ordinate the character and proportions of the *Poem*, we complete our definition of the perfect Epic as the expression of a perfect human mind by means of one beautiful or sublime truth, and other essentially related truths, arranged according to their essential relationship, *in a proportioned succession of words true and congruous, and therefore sublime or beautiful.* A perfect Poem would be therefore a miniature of the Creation not in its matter but its principles; the Kosmos not of God but Man; the humanization of abstract Truth; the soul, as it were, become concrete; the word of Man made flesh and dwelling amongst us; and being the expression of the highest state to which the whole human mind can attain on Earth it would be limited to no era or nation but would be accepted and understood in its fullness whenever, at however vast an interval of history, another human mind anywhere attained the same elevation, and less and less partially and obscurely as each of us in the development of our best qualities rose nearer to the hopeless pinnacle of that supreme immaculate height.

Having ascertained the principles of a *Perfect* Poem we may safely lay down of Poems that they are right in so far as they consist with this type and wrong in so far as they recede from it : and of poetry that it is excellent in so far as it could form part of such perfect Poem and imperfect in so far as it is incongruous therewith.

Before proceeding to a closer investigation of some of the separate parts of which Poetry—perfect or imperfect—is composed, two questions naturally present themselves which it will be well to answer here where they arise. The one is 'if a perfect Poem be the outcome of a perfect mind what chance is there of our ever having such a Poem?'

The other 'how is it that men who have written unquestionable poetry have been as men so very far from perfection?'

The answer to these questions brings us, I believe, to the secret of all great Poems and of some of the most perplexing problems of Poetry. There are among men an order of minds gifted with the power of—I am of course using the word with no reference to its Scriptural meaning—transfiguration.

We are familiar with an inferior form of the gift in the bodily transformation of which some men are capable, so as to assume, as it were, the features and gait of another : and we see a subordinate manifestation of the gift itself in the case of the great Actor, and a diseased and involuntary exhibition of its phenomena in the hallucinations of the Lunatic.

The higher forms of this gift enable the possessor to re-construct (so to speak) his whole character into that of some other mind.

In such persons the process is instinctive, and as the Actor cannot tell you by what laws he reproduces the face and manner of his hero, neither can he who has in the highest form the gift whereof we speak explain the process of its action.

A single look often suffices to give the actor his bodily cue: a word, a thought, a feeling may be sufficient for the mental transformation of the Poet. In this transformation the proportionate activity of his various qualities is so much altered that the proportion of the inherent qualities themselves seems, for the time being, changed: attributes that were large and notable become insignificant, and those that were in comparative abeyance during ordinary life arise into signal and masterful exercise. The possession of this gift does not make a man a Poet, but I think no imperfect Man can be a great Poet without possessing it. When possessed by one otherwise fitted to be a Poet it has two principal modes of manifestation. The one—and primary—is that at any beautiful or sublime influence it transfigures the mind towards Perfection—approaching the perfect state in proportion to its own power in the given mind and the

nature of the mental materials on which it has to work :
—in this state the Poem is designed. The second is
that in representing the human characters of the Poem it
transfigures the mind into those characters for the time
being—and by a succession of such states the characteriz-
ation of the Poem is executed. The amount of completeness in this second transfiguration makes one
difference between the Epic and the Drama.

The Epic being like some Dramatic story told by a
great Tragedian wherein his successive but partial im-
personations of the different characters meet in the permanent unity of himself, the one narrator; and the
Drama the action of the same story enacted by him *en
costume*, without the narrative, and with no central
figure of himself in which the various dissimilar personi-
fications might unite and cohere. A Poet has therefore
a world—the world of imagined facts—of infinite possible
variety, and an inexhaustible stock of men and women in
the transmutable substance of his own character : and by
the peculiarity of his nature the environments of this
imaginary world affect him as actual circumstances affect
ordinary men, and he lives, for a time, in these men and
women as naturally as in his own personality. Out of
this world and from these men and women he has to
select and construct his Poem. The primary character

of the individual Poet and the degree to which he possesses the transfiguring power will determine the character of the Poem and regulate its approach to perfection. Where Love predominates the Lyric will be its expression in modes of predominating Beauty, and in the Epic the main subject will be Beautiful : where Worship the Lyric will be reverent and sublime and the Epic will take a subject of awe or terror : and in proportion to the sense of truth and relation the materials of the Poem will be more or less just and the ordination of it more or less perfect. In the highest type of Poet the Lyric will be the expression of combined Love and Reverence, and the subject chosen for the Epic will be at once Beautiful and Sublime.

Having thus come down from the heights of that perfect Ideal which we are not likely to see realized, to those regions of the possible which human poets may hope to climb, and to the topmost ledges of which they have now and then ascended, let us look, in the light of the general principles I have been endeavouring to set forth, more minutely at some of the peculiarities of all poetic expression. We have seen that as a Poem is the expression of a Poet's mind, every portion of a Poem, from the Epic to the single passage, is the result of the same principles, almost as we see in the beautiful science of crystallography that the whole crystal is but a larger atom. Let us take one of the poetic atoms for analysis. We shall be met at the onset by the question 'how if the whole Poem be but an equivalent to the Poet's mind, can the single passage be an equivalent to the same characteristics?'

This is readily explained by an inward glance at the manner of our mental activities.

Take for instance our whole power to love.

We shall find the total Love of which we are capable to be like the Ocean, which though it be one water yet by meeting and incalculably crossing forces—invariable sway of the rolling globe, variable beat of all manner of winds, Sun-stroke, and Moon-stroke, actions, reactions, and interactions, multiplied past mortal skill, of waves, tides, shores, promontories, reefs, and rivers,—is roused into innumerable apparitions of the same substance, each having the form of separation without the power thereof, each diverse as to its momentary manifestation but indifferent as to its permanent nature, and holding, for its own space and season, the same shapeless, motionless, colourless, general element in a special moving, figured, coloured individuality. Now these billows, ripples, flakes and drops of a great general feeling or other attribute have, when they can be expressed at all, each for itself correlatives in the external world, and by the serial expression of this temporary *personæ* the great flood finds, as it were, its narrow way by the straits of successional utterance. And thus, though no single fact of the imagination may be able, in the words of our great Poet, to 'take up the whole of Love and utter it,' the Poet, through his ordinating power, creates by the ordered assemblage of forms individually beautiful, an organized whole of Beauty sufficient for the Whole of Love, and corresponding in its parts to the vibrations of its successional activity. What is true in the case of Love, has analogous truth in the activity of the other mental powers.

Let us therefore out of that organized imaginative Whole which the Poet has produced take any one of the complete facts of Imagination whereof it is made up, and examine its constituents. Under the simplest conditions of expression, the expressed fact must consist of itself and the words that express it. As we have seen that it must itself be either beautiful or sublime, it corresponds to the Poet's love or worship. Proceeding outwards from the mind, you have therefore, first the fact, the equivalent of a feeling, and then the words, the equivalent of the fact.

And as the truth of the fact is the equivalent of the faculty to know, and the relationship of the fact to the feeling and the words to the fact, the equivalent of that sense of relation which is the characteristic of the power to order, you have in the single expressed fact what you had in the great combination of such facts, the Poem, an equivalent for to feel, to know, and to order.

This is an instance of the simplest kind: proceed to one more difficult. Suppose the fact of the imagination is one that has no equivalent in words, or that from familiarity, popular misuse, or double meanings, its original verbal signs are no longer poetic equivalents. Suppose you have to express such a fact. You must find for that fact an equivalent in some other fact that has an equivalent in words. An equivalent is, as we have seen, something which being presented to the quiet mind will produce there the thing of which it is the equivalent. You require therefore a fact that shall produce in the mind another fact; you require something more, a fact that shall produce a beautiful or sublime fact; and yet something more, a fact that shall produce such a fact in a mind whose primary characteristics are a sense of truth and a sense of relation. Your equivalent, therefore, must truly and essentially correspond to the beautiful or sublime fact for which it stands. That it does so makes it not only an equivalent for that fact but for your sense of truth and relationship. And as that first fact was an equivalent to certain feelings, this second fact not only stands for the first, but stands also for your characteristics of feeling, knowing and ordering. Now a fact that thus stands for another is its metaphor. We have arrived therefore at this law of all metaphor—that every true metaphor is not only a metaphor of the thing for which it stands but of *the Poet who placed it*.

Time does not allow me to multiply instances and to carry out the principle into still more minute detail, but I think, if at leisure you examine any variety of examples, you will find that this is the law of all poetic equivalents and that it explains those erroneous figures of speech which are so often mistaken for Poetry. What are critically called concetti, or conceits, and those misperceptions of Nature which arise from what an eminent writer has lately denominated 'the pathetic fallacy,' and those substitutions of horrors for terrors and the carnal for the human which we call melodrama, are the equivalents of minds in whom, either constitutionally, or for the time being, there is something wrong in the kind or the balance of the powers to love, to worship, to know and to order.

Having formed our poetic passage in the imagination—having found for our feelings metaphors in facts and for our unspeakable facts metaphors in facts that have corresponding words, the remainder of the act of expression would not need examination if words were arbitrary signs. But, as we all know, (however much philologers may differ about the precise primitive roots and their values,) there can be no doubt that in the first origin of language all words were metaphors—that is had an essential relationship to the facts for which they stood. And since every word of our modern languages is the result of some modification, combination, and recombination of those primitives, something of the essential relationship must still exist. But since those modifications and combinations have often taken place under the control of very artificial conditions, and since in the lapse of ages the various conditioning forces have crossed and recrossed into a complexity not often to be unravelled, the consciousness of original relation is so far lost that the words of a modern language are neither algebraic signs nor metaphorical equivalents, but range between these extremes and frequently approach either. In such a language (since he must not create a new one) the Poet has to express himself. In it he must find an equivalent for his imagined facts. We have seen the laws of poetic equivalents. An arbitrary sign does not fulfil those laws. The Poet requires his equivalent to be not a sign but a metaphor, *and the whole action of his mind on language is therefore to elevate it from the sign towards the metaphor.*

The first result of this action is to instinctively select from the mass of verbal signs those words that retain most of their old essential relation to the thing signified. The next is to impart to them what shall, as far as may be, restore what is lost of that relation : to make them essentially akin to the facts they represent. Now one of the proofs that two apparently different things agree is the identity of their effects. If I strike you, successively, with a rod of iron, of silver, and of gold, it will seem at first sight indeed that one effect is produced by very different causes : but on closer enquiry we shall see that the pain produced was neither because the producing rod was iron, silver, or gold, but because it was hard, and that the iron, silver, and gold produced the same pain because they agreed in being *hard*. Identical effects are therefore evidence of relationship in the causes, and when such effects occur in such a mind as we are investigating identical effects are the evidence of *essential* relationship. The Poet therefore adds to his selected words something which by having the same effect as the fact for which they stand shows itself to be essentially related to that fact. That 'something' is *rhythm*.

Words rhythmically combined affect the feelings of the poetic hearer or utterer in the same way as the fact they represent : and thus by a reflex action the fact is reproduced in the imagination. By instinctive selection and rhythmic combination the verbal utterance is thus elevated from a sign to or towards a metaphor, and becomes, like other metaphors, not only a metaphor of the proximate poetic fact *but of the characteristics of the Poet.*

We saw a little while ago that the law of the whole Epic, that it is one subject with its congruous accessories, must apply to every passage of which the Epic is made up. We have now seen by an analysis of one such passage that the other law of the whole Epic, that it should be a metaphor of the Poet's characteristics, is not only fulfilled in every passage, but in every cardinal portion of a passage : in every complete act of expression and in the sub-acts of which it is composed. Carrying out the homology of the whole and the parts, let us now, reasoning from the less to the greater, by one more examination of the passage explain a difficulty in the Epic. Select a complete expression and pull it to pieces. I will take a well-known saying of Shakspeare because it not only illustrates what I am going to say, but also happens to be exemplary of a truth I have just now been bringing before you. Othello, bending over Desdemona and prefiguring what he is going to do, says not, 'when I have killed thee,' but 'when I have plucked thy rose.'

Here you have an instance in which the fact of the

imagination had no equivalent in words, and had to be expressed by another fact for which such an equivalent existed. That somewhat by which the living differed from the dead,—that wonder of vital form and colour, that visible presence of thought and passion, that fragrant atmosphere of sweet influences, that spiritual mystery of an incarnate soul by which she was not a corpse but *Desdemona*, had not—and will never have—a name or phrase among men. But in the language of God there was a fact essentially akin to it for which we had a human sign; the Poet instinctively turned to that equivalent, and the ineffable became effable in a Rose. But I quote this sentence 'when I have plucked thy rose' that having perceived its surpassing beauty as a whole you may take it in pieces and so, to use its own metaphor, 'pluck the rose' of it. For that somewhat by which the whole sentence lives, and the parts live while forming a whole, is like the living Desdemona, something not to be defined. 'When I have plucked thy rose,' separate those words altogether from the general idea and restrict them to their several utterly independent meanings. You will find that they have all expired a something with which they before were warm, and that some of them, 'when' and 'have' for instance, are almost without any life or significance at all. Look out 'when' and the auxiliary verb 'to have' in the Dictionary and see how empty and effete they are. Now reunite the sentence, and behold the same 'when' and the same 'have' full, and brimming over, with the life, colour, and beauty of the whole.

Now this circulation of vitality and beauty from the whole into its parts which you have seen in the single sentence, takes place also in the total Epic and explains how some members of a great Poem—as it were the prepositions and conjunctions of that mighty syntax—which taken separately do not seem to express either the Love or Worship of the Poet are, nevertheless, by their essential union with wholes of which they are perceived by his peculiar gifts to be necessary parts, and of whose essence they are therefore partakers, as truly the fulfilment of the great primary Poetic Law as the most dazzling centres of the Beautiful or the Sublime.

We have now in endeavouring to find the principles of Perfect Poetry investigated a perfect Poem in its origin, its wholes, and its parts. We have enquired into the Principles of the producing Mind, into the Principles of the total thing produced, and all the members which compose it, and we have discovered the human means by which its production becomes possible to imperfect humanity. We have found a Poem to be from first to last, in things and in words, *the manifold metaphor of a human mind*, and to approach perfection within and without, in spirit and in matter, in design and execution, in the ratio wherein the mind of whose activity it is the equivalent is *at the time of its production* perfect.

To elaborate these general truths into all their completeness would require a whole season of Lectures, but I would remind you, in passing, that whereas we have been compelled to confine ourselves this evening to a mere sketch of the main characteristics of the Poet and of his work, the perfect Poem should really be the equivalent of his whole nature, the expression of every quality by which he is truly, though ideally, human.

I have explained at the commencement of these remarks why in proposing a standard of Poetry I chose the ideal and perfect Poet and Poem as they might exist instead of the real and imperfect Poet and Poem as they are actually known to us. But it may be asked why, instead of going into the principles of such Ideals, have I not contented myself with bringing before you such selected passages from existing poems as may be held faultless, or with giving a brief sketch of such Poems as I supposed to be most nearly perfect? To this I answer that inasmuch as the value of a just notion of Poetry is not only that we may be able to identify it when seen in full flowered Perfection, but that as Critics we may be able to estimate it rightly when—as in the majority of instances—we catch it in manifestations not wholly mature, the knowledge of Principles is even of more importance than that of their supreme results. For as in morals so in Poetry it is not he who mechanically copies the *actions*, but he who vitally—in the best mode possible to his given stage of development—applies the *principles* of the Perfect Character that really most resembles it in nature.

There is a poetical as well as a moral hypocrisy : and it is possible for the literary as well as the moral Pharisee to make void the living Law through dead tradition. You remember some Sir Galahad or Sir Tristram of old who passed in armour his years of heroic gentleness and sought, sword in hand, the sangreal of Purity and Truth. Some Knight without fear and without reproach, who met his enemy as a brother, and nursed him with a Lover's chivalrous devotion, and who falling himself after a thousand triumphs had such words as these said over his noble corse :

 ''Thou wert the courteousest Knight that ever bore shield; thou wert the truest friend that ever bestrode horse ; thou wert the truest Lover that ever loved woman; thou wert the kindest man that ever struck with sword ; thou wert the goodliest person that ever came among press of Knights; thou wert the meekest man and the gentlest that ever ate in hall with ladies ; and thou wert the sternest Knight to thy mortal foe that ever laid lance in rest.'

You can also perhaps remember (he was to be found, occasionally, a year or two back), some nineteenth century advocate of philosophical pacification, who loves God with £. s. d. and his customer as himself, who answers with a perverted text the cry of the weak and the oppressed, and refutes the Patriot's heart with irrefragable arithmetic ; who is so jealous of his country's blood that he would keep it for her blushes ; and—holding Life more precious than all that is beautiful to live for—would fill his pockets in the name of Christian amity with that worst bribe of Tyrants, the prosperity of dishonour. There can be no doubt which of these two is the least warlike ; but I ask you which is really nearer to the Gospel of Love and Peace?

It was necessary, therefore, in order to estimate imperfect Poets and Poetry, that we should investigate the *principles* even more than the *practice* of the Perfect. Having dealt in what is past with the ideal, I purpose in the short remainder of this lecture to glance briefly at the real. I have developed the premiss with which we started, that 'a perfect Poem is the perfect expression of a perfect human mind,' into an hypothesis as to perfect

Poetry and perfect Poets; I will now, if you please, proceed to illustrate the principal propositions of that hypothesis by the acknowledged facts of Poetry and Poets as they exist. As that hypothesis was, I think, a sober and legitimate deduction, I shall by demonstrating its conclusions, arrive at something like a proof of the premiss. My first proposition was, in effect, that a perfect Poet is a man possessing in the highest degree these gifts—to love, and its accompaniment the sense of Beauty, to worship, and its accompaniment the sense of the Sublime, to order, and its accompaniment the sense of Relation, and to know, or that ability of perceiving Truth without which the other gifts would have no proper objects of exercise. Now let us see what, by universal consent, have been the characteristics of imperfect Poets who have actually existed, and see how far they go towards our theory of the perfect. But you may meet me by the objection that common consent is valueless with regard to qualities that are supposed to be beyond the judgment of the majority of mankind. The objection, if valid, is valid also, more or less, with regard to all the highest and rarest objects of human thought. But I would suggest in the present case a mode of arriving at truth which, while neither wholly popular nor wholly private, combines the advantages of both without the evils of either, and unites that guarantee of general humanity which is only contained in common consent with those advantages of special aptitude, which by the fact of its speciality, must always in all cases, be the privilege of the few.

The process is based on the general facts, admitted on all sides, that however different in amount and intensity our different mental powers may be in different individuals, they are possessed in some degree by the whole of Mankind : and that, as resulting from this community, there are some things on which the whole race are agreed.

The process in its most familiar form is this,—and in the less familiar form in which it can be publicly used, it is essentially the same. Taking one of these common consents—as that grass is green, or sunshine beautiful, consider *who* among your friends seems most—and most continually—impressed with this fact on which all agree. Ask that person whom, of all he knows, he considers a greater judge of green, or of beauty, than himself. Apply to that third for his superior in the same line, and so persevere till from the base of a common consent you rise to the pinnacle of a consummate individual knowledge.

This is the true intellectual democracy, wherein the many are made *not the judge*, but the means of *discovering* the judge.

It does not follow that it is also the true political democracy, because, for one reason among others— æsthetics seeks the perennial and absolute *best*, and politics has to do with the relative and the temporary.

Now applying this method to · the enquiry in hand, and leaving, of course, the sacred Writers out of the question, whom should we discover by this graduated ascent to be the ultimate supreme appeal in all questions of the Beautiful? Undoubtedly, in every land where Poetry has existed, some Poet.

Of the Sublime? Some Poet.

Of Truth—in that sense whereof we have been speaking—from the time when the Greek said ἀείδω— I see intensely - for 'I sing,' to the day that Wordsworth saw and sang the Celandine and the Daisy? Some Poet.

Of order—that harmony and melody which in their best known manifestation of *Music* have taken their very name from *the Muse*,—that proportion which has made 'to lisp in numbers' a proverb for Poetry, that ordinated Wholeness which gave title alike to the Greek ποιητής, and the Scottish *Makar*, and which has lent us the phrase of Epic Unity as our highest expression of a multiform *One*? Some Poet.

And what process do we need for arriving at the testimony to that worship by which, in every land, the

Poets have filled earth, air, and sky, with mythologies; peopled at once Asgard, Hades, and Olympus, crowded on the heights of Bifrost the sons of Muspel and the einheriar of Odin, drawn round the violet-crowned city its thirty thousand gods—gods that this day and while the world lasts, hold for awful Pallas the siege with time and Ruin—or

>   Dum Capitolium
> Scandet cum tacitâ virgine Pontifex,

have seated Jove on the eternity of his consecrated hill? And we need no formal evidence of that universal Poet's *Love*, high as Heaven, deep even as Hell, wide not only as Creation, but as the difference between Created and Creator:—that Love which, whether singing least or greatest, first or last, matter or spirit, temporal or eternal— the dewdrop or the ocean, the flower or the star, the glint of a glowworm or the splendour of Noon, the choir of Angels or the minstrelsy of Birds, the beauty of the loftiest Queen of Sheba, or the eyes of the poorest outcast that ever trembled with a penitent tear, the coloured glory of the summer world, or the incandent Wonder of the Great White Throne, the robe of morning, buckled with the Sun, or those other skirts 'dark with excess of light'—so sang that Prophets have been content to set their message to such music, and that wherever since Men were upon Earth, love to God or love to man has been bursting a human bosom, the dumb humanity that must speak or die, has snatched some Poet's harp and saved itself in Poetry.

I could have wished to exemplify these qualities to which the consent of Mankind testifies, by reading from the works of ancients and moderns, some of those many specimens of the Sublime and Beautiful on which we are agreed.

But time compels me to hasten on.

Before illustrating the proposition that a perfect Poem is the perfect expression of such a mind as we have been examining, let me draw your attention for a moment to the other truths regarding expression itself; and first that a perfect expression is that product of an active and perfect mind, which, being brought into contact *with the same mind* in a passive state, would restore the state of which it is the expression.

At first sight I know you would be inclined to say 'that product of an active mind which being brought into contact with *another* mind, would produce that state whereof it is the expression:' but a little examination will show us that as soon as the expressor leaves the test of his own consciousness he loses the ground of all certitude, and not only subjects himself to a gamut of criteria wide as the space between a European and a Bosjesman, and among Europeans between a Newton and a gamin, but has no power even to ascertain in any precise manner whether he answers those criteria or not. And a little further consideration will show us that the value of that ideal and perfect standard we have taken depends on its being the common measure of every part of that to which we apply it : and we shall perceive that the characteristic homogeneity of a perfect Poem, and of perfect Poetry, is the result of its conformity—intrinsic and extrinsic—to this single standard.

These facts afford a solution to the long vexed problem of the difference between Rhetoric and Poetry. That difference has puzzled the majority of investigators, because they have sought it not in *cause* but in *effect*,— in the thing produced and not in the mode of production. The things produced sometimes, in given selected instances, do not differ : the invariable difference is in the mode of production. Poetry is, as we have seen, the expression of a mind according to its own laws. Rhetoric is the expression of a mind according to the laws of its Hearer.

Poetry is the human embodiment of Truth in that form which is essentially truest to the Truth embodied.

Rhetoric, even in the best sense, is the embodiment

of it in that form which is most affecting to certain Beholders. The Rhetor addresses his audience ; and is estimated by his power over them at a given time and place.

The Poet addresses no audience, and is known by his power, in every age and land while mankind exists, over minds that approach the type of his own representative Humanity.

It may happen regarding the works of the Rhetor and the Poet, that at certain points their orbits intersect, but watch them awhile, and as surely as in obedience to inexorable causes, two stars meet, pass, and depart on opposite paths, you shall see that they deviate into wide and wider separation—ay, and perhaps that, like those stars, the fact of their momentary conjunction was an evidence of the contrariety of the forces by which they moved.

A perfect poetic expression then is, that which being brought into contact with the passive mind of the expressor, will restore the state of which it is the expression—and this I have called an equivalent. That things may be the equivalents of feelings is proved by examples which will occur spontaneously to the minds of all of us. Merely glancing at those innumerable instances which might be drawn from the plastic arts, from Religious and other ceremonies, from devotional and monumental architecture, and all the other visible representatives of the passions, let me draw your notice a moment to a well known illustration in modern sculpture—Thorwaldsen's famous marble of 'Night.' You remember the great Mother flying in her sleep, with vast wings and drooping head; bearing two sleeping babes, like two poppy buds, in her breast, and followed by an owl. The four are *Night*; not either one but the total four. There is no phenomenal likeness to Night in the group, and if you try to separate them the resemblance is, if possible, less. For Night is motionless,—but the Woman is evidently moving: nevertheless, her bent head and the gravitating lines in the Babes, so visibly heavy with slumber, neutralize the sense of motion and make it seem *a less effort to move than to stand still.* Again Night is silent, yet those giant pinions of hers cannot surely flap without a rush of noise; but the owl behind them, 'the muffled bird of noiseless flight,' whose large wings will pass your ear as silent as a butterfly, takes out, as it were, the sound from the whole sculpture, and reduces it to a total of Truth.

But how 'a total of Truth,' for Night is black and they are whitest marble: Night is shapeless and they are all exquisite shapes: Night is mainly negative and they are positive throughout.

A total Truth nevertheless, because, phenomenally different as the things may be, you *feel* when looking on the Sculpture as you *feel* when looking upon Night. The Sculpture is the equivalent of your feeling, your feeling —on the principle I explained in treating of rhythm— creates by reflex action, the fact of Night in the imagination; Night and the Sculpture are metaphors of each other by being common metaphors of a single state of mind. Did time permit I might illustrate the equivalence of things to feelings in another department of Art by reading an exquisite song of Tennyson's which you all remember—'Break, break, break, on thy cold grey stones, oh sea!': a song which is, as a whole, the mere metaphor of a mental attitude that every one can understand, that no one could scientifically define, but that is more or less reproduced in the reader by the images which the Poet sets afloat in the imagination.

My proposition that the great law of Poetic equivalents is this, that every Poetic metaphor is not only a metaphor of the thing metaphorized but of the Poet, in other words, that every metaphor must be essentially, and not merely accidentally, related to the thing for which it stands, and that every perfect Poetic Metaphor must also be either beautiful or sublime, you may readily illustrate by a comparison between the art and the symbolism of various times and peoples. The Christ of mediæval Religious Art was the *metaphor*, and the well-known fish-symbol—chosen, you know, because the word ἰχθύς was supposed to contain the initial letters of His titles—was *not* the metaphor of the Saviour because one had essential and the other only accidental relations to Him.

The Ceres of Greek art *was*, and the many-breasted goddess of Hindoo symbolism was *not*, the poetic metaphor of fruitful Nature, because the first was true and beautiful, the second only similar and ugly.

The Snowdrop, because it fulfils all the poetic laws, is a metaphor of maidenhood; but a ring on the first finger is only the sign of it, because it arises out of other than essential relations. In the same way compare as equivalents of Love the Venus of Melos or of Medici, with some Indian Image of Kam Deo or with the symbolism of a Valentine. Or compare the ancient hieroglyphic writing, in which the sign pictured the thing signified, with the later hieroglyph in which the sign stood not for the thing but for the first sound in the name of the thing, or with the alphabet of modern times, in which almost the last trace of metaphor is lost.

Finally, compare the sublime metaphor of Scripture, 'God is Light,' with those effigies of the Deity which shock us in some mediæval paintings, and with those mathematical definitions within which the ancient Scholasticism sought to shut up Him Whom the Heaven of Heavens cannot contain.

In these true metaphors, and in all other cases of true poetic metaphor, we shall find a recognition of something more than a phenomenal similarity; we shall find the type and antitype, like two lines that meet somewhere but not here, slanting towards some common truth far back in the profounds of causation,—some truth in its unity unseen and for ever invisible, but, in the relationship of its remote diverging issues, *felt*, as the blind needle feels the pole, by the total perception of a consummate human mind. Recognizing thus the deep mystery that is in every true metaphor we raise it from the rank of ornament to a solemn significance, and understand the wisdom of the saying of Aristotle—'the greatest thing is to employ metaphors well for this alone cannot be acquired from another but is an indication of an excellent Genius.' And perceiving moreover that the law of the metaphor is really that of all poetic expression, and that the Poem is therefore a metaphor of the human soul, we recognize in Poetry that reconciliation of Spirit and Matter, of the inward and the outward, which no effort of voluntary reason can achieve, but which is accomplished, as all our necessities that transcend the powers of reason are accomplished, by an instrument specially created for that end.

Viewing the Poet as that instrument, that great and curious Divine Machine, strong as the forces of Nature, but more sensitive than any Æolian string that ever trembled to an imperceptible wind, one is reminded of the old Ptolemæan story of the Gygonian rock which could not be removed from its place by any human power, but could be stirred, therein, by the stalk of an Asphodel. And when perplexed for the secondary causes by which the instrument performs its God-appointed Work one turns involuntarily to other mysteries of Providence and recalls such natural marvels as Professor Wilson showed us, not long since, in his lecture upon colours, when rays so apparently different as the chemical and the luminous—rays that even to the delicate nerves of the eye gave nothing but symptoms of diversity —were discovered by a still finer test to be essentially the same, and that which had passed through ordinary substances as darkness in one specially-adapted medium became light.

In treating of that last stage of poetic expression by which *things* have their equivalents in *words*, I proposed to you that the necessary effect of what we had recognised as the Poet's characteristics would be the elevation of even the *words* of poetic speech towards the rank of *metaphor*, by securing an *essential* likeness between the sign and the thing signified : and that one of the great means of this elevation was *rhythm*. That certain quantities and accents in connected words—certain modes of verbal *motion*, involving a certain direct action of the organs of speech and hearing, and a sympathetic action in the rest of the system—bodily and mental—in other terms that certain *rhythms* and measures are metaphors of ideas and feelings I will illustrate by a few well-known examples, which I have taken chiefly from Authors not English in order that you may the more readily forget—as I must request you to forget—altogether the sense of the individual words and attend only to the effect of the rhythmic combination.

The first is the famous line from Homer in which the heavy stone that has been rolled to the hill-top rebounds to the bottom

Αὖτις ἔπειτα πέδονδε κυλίνδετο λᾶας ἀναιδής.

Any one who has sat on a hill and pushed a stone over the precipitous brow will recognize in the marvellous measure of this line the whole history of the descent. Αὖτις—it rolls lazily over the brow,—ἔπειτα—stung by the first jag of rock it leaps from the earth ;—rebounding from a midway ledge—πέτονδε—it has sprung like a planet into mid-air :—now touching the first slopes of the plain see how—round and hardly visible—it whirls like a wheel in κυλίνδετο—; and thrown back, like a cannon shot from yonder strong wall in the flat, finishes at last in λᾶας ἀναιδής.

Take the contrary fact in Milton's description of the toilsome upheaval of the great Mass from the hill-foot to the top.

> So he with difficulty and labour hard
> Toiled on with difficulty and labour he.

I would refer you at your leisure to the celebrated bow-shot in Homer, the fall of the bull, and the labour of the Cyclops in Virgil, the flight of Alcyone in Ovid and the dancing measures of the Greek Tragedians.

> Ἔκλαγξαν δ' ἄρ ὀϊστοὶ ἐπ' ὤμων χωομένοιο.
> Δεινὴ δὲ κλαγγὴ γένετ' ἀργυρέοιο βιοῖο.
> Sternitur exanimisque tremens procumbit humi bos.
> Illi inter sese magna vi brachia tollunt.
> Percutiensque levem modo natis aëra pennis,
> Stringebat summas ales miserabilis undas.
>
> MET. b. xi. 733-34.

I quote the Schoolboy's favourite line of the galloping Horse in Virgil,

> Quadrupedante putrem sonitu quatit ungula campum.

because it has a modern parallel in the marvellous rhythm

of our own Laureate in which the light cavalry still gallop to glory at Balaclava.

> Half a league, half a league, half a league onward.

The fall of Lucifer in Dante's Purgatorio is a noble example

> Giù dal cielo
> Folgoreggiando scendere, da un lato.

And the fall of a body in the Inferno in which the heavy helpless clamp with which a corpse falls flattened on a floor tells its story in utter independence of the literal sense.

> E caddi, come corpo morto cade.

And as an example of an opposite kind I will beg you to read, what I wish time permitted me to quote, and to surrender yourselves, irrespective of the sense, to the bacchanalian rhythm of Francesco Redi's 'Bacco in Toscana.'

Among other means of elevating the verbal sign to the rank of metaphor the choice of words in which there is a relation of sound and sense is frequent in the Poetry of every language. That this choice is governed by the same laws that rule all other metaphors—that the resemblance must be one not of mere sensuous similarity but of essential relation—I would illustrate by referring you to the suggestions of the cries of animals and birds in Beethoven's pastoral symphony, and in Meyerbeer's Prelude to the Prophet, and to imitations of the same things by birdcalls and other mimetic machinery; and by contrasting Milton's trumpet line—

> Sonorous metal blowing martial sound,

with Swift's

> Tantara, tantara, while all the boy's holloa,

or by opposing Virgil's cooing line of turtle doves,

> Nec tamen interea raucæ, tua cura, palumbes—

or verses in Shelley's Skylark and Coleridge's Nightingale to the more phenomenally accurate, but less essentially true, representation of the thrush and blackbird in the clever jeux d'esprit of William Allingham.

My propositions as to the unity of subject in a perfect Poem, and as to the (to use a physiological term) *homotypy* of every natural member of that Poem, are the necessary results of what I have taken to be the conditions of human perception. Those conditions are not inconsistent, I think, with either of our foremost systems of philosophy, are supported by that congruity of mind and body which science and Philosophy alike demonstrate, and have the unconscious testimony of the idiom of all ages and languages. I think, therefore, I need not here enter into proof of that congruity, and may assume the conditions as already proved. As both my propositions are the logical inferences from these conditions, and as the first of them merely accounts for facts on which we are all agreed (for the unity of the epical subject has been the axiom of all criticism), I will leave you to test them at your leisure, by any number of examples—especially as they apply to all human expression, and only in a peculiar manner to Poetry as it should be the most perfect form of that expression.

The proposition which contains the *modus operandi* by which the imperfect Poet rises on the one hand towards the ideally perfect mind and descends on the other to the varieties of common human character, is also not of a nature to need detailed demonstration here. Though very important in itself the facts for which it accounts are at once too numerous and too well-known for quotation.

The means by which Poets of no wide external experience, and few opportunities, therefore, of taking the moral portraits, line by line, of men as they are, can fill their scenes with every type and variety of Mankind, astonish the traveller, the soldier, the statesman, the physician, by pictures as accurate as their own eyesight, and startle the highest King or the lowest Beggar, the sturdiest Manhood, or the tenderest Woman, with the very inmost revelations of themselves, is a problem which each of us must often have tried to solve. The hypothesis that the Poet has the power to *become*, for the time, King or Beggar, Man or Woman, and, when thus transformed, to feel imagined scenes as the rest of us feel actual circumstances, accounts, I think, for the phenomena to be explained, and is not inconsistent with other established truths. From the boys who erred on one side when they cried after Dante, 'lo the man who was in Hell,' to the passer-by who erred as far on the other when he fancied he saw the Poet of the Lakes in that William Wordsworth who was chaffering for a penny with the carrier at his door, all Poetical Biography has been one long perplexing contrast of the Man and the Artist, and all Poems have been, more or less, untrue to that poor mortal whose name men saw upon the title page.

We have at length done with the Poet's mind, and the nature and laws of its expression.

I now, in conclusion, briefly proceed to the proposition that a Poem is the characteristic expression of such a mind, and that Poetry is that which can congruously form part of such a Poem. As it would take many lectures to array before you the great Poems of the World, and so illustrate my case, I will take a method more manageable, and I think sufficiently convincing, and let you see with your own eyes the dry bones of fact become the living Apollo of Poetry.

Taking an acknowledged Poetic subject, the Coliseum at Rome, I will read to you first the simple statistics of its shape, size, et cetera. I will then read a description of the same object by a poetic but not a Poet's mind, in which the bare statistical skeleton is clothed upon with some *beauty, sublimity, and relation*; and finally I will read Byron's memorable lines, in which feelings, facts, and relationships have arranged themselves in *rhythmical equivalents* at once, in idea and in word, true, beautiful, and sublime.

Here are the statistics.

'This Ampitheatre is in form an ellipse. Its superficial area is nearly six acres: its major axis 620 feet, its minor axis 513: the present height of its outer wall 157. Of this circuit scarcely a half presents its original height, and throughout a great portion of it the travertine arcades are demolished, and the rough wall inside, partially erect, is overgrown with grass and shrubs and covered by a modern support. The centre is occupied by the oval arena 287 feet long by 180 wide.

'Round the arena, and resting on a huge mass of arches rising on arches, the sloping seats for the spectators (of which the building could contain 87,000) ascend towards the summit of the external wall.'

Here the same thing with a sense of something more than the physical facts. (From Joseph Forsyth 'On Antiquities, Arts and Letters in Italy.')

'As it now stands, the Coliseum is a striking image of Rome itself: decayed—vacant—serious—yet grand;—half grey and half green—erect on one side and fallen on the other, with consecrated ground in its bosom—inhabited by a beadsman; visited by every caste; for moralists, antiquaries, architects, devotees, all meet here to meditate, to examine, to draw, to measure, and to pray. "In contemplating antiquities," says Livy, "the mind itself becomes antique." It contracts from such objects a venerable rust, which I prefer to the polish and the point of those wits who have lately profaned this august ruin with ridicule.'

Here the Poetry of the whole.

> 'The stars are forth, the moon above the tops
> Of the snow-shining mountains. Beautiful!
> I linger yet with Nature, for the night
> Hath been to me a more familiar face
> Than that of man; and in her starry shade
> Of dim and solitary loveliness,
> I learn'd the language of another world.

'I do remember me, that in my youth,
When I was wandering—upon such a night
I stood within the Coliseum's wall,
Midst the chief relics of almighty Rome.
The trees which grew along the broken arches
Waved dark in the blue midnight, and the stars
Shone through the rents of ruin ; from afar
The watch-dog bay'd beyond the Tiber ; and
More near from out the Cæsar's palace came
The owl's long cry, and, interruptedly,
Of distant sentinels the fitful song
Began and died upon the gentle wind.
Some cypresses beyond the time-worn breach
Appear'd to skirt the horizon, yet they stood
Within a bowshot. Where the Cæsars dwelt,
And dwell the tuneless birds of night, amidst
A grove which springs through levell'd battlements,
And twines its roots with the imperial hearths,
Ivy usurps the laurel's place of growth :—
But the gladiator's bloody Circus stands,
A noble wreck in ruinous perfection !
While Cæsar's chambers and the Augustan halls,
Grovel on earth in indistinct decay.
And thou didst shine, thou rolling moon, upon
All this, and cast a wide and tender light,
Which soften'd down the hoar austerity
Of rugged desolation, and fill'd up,
As 'twere anew, the gaps of centuries ;
Leaving that beautiful which still was so,
And making that which was not, till the place
Became religion, and the heart ran o'er
With silent worship of the great of old !
The dead, but sceptered sovereigns, who still rule
Our spirits from their urns.'—MANFRED.

I would recommend you to try a similar experiment with the death of King Arthur in the glorious old legend and

Tennyson's wonderful idealization of it in the 'Morte d'Arthur.'[1]

Having thus in the course of this Lecture descended from a general primary hypothesis to its detailed inferences and, afterwards, from an observation of facts, ascended through those details to the origin of the hypothesis—having endeavoured to show that it is consistent with itself, that it explains the phenomena to be accounted for, and is not incongruous with established truths,—I will close by pointing out in very few words, two particulars wherein, as it seems to me, this hypothesis is singularly fortunate. The first is that while, so far as I know, wholly contained by no previous theory, it admits, explains and unites into itself the best theories of the best Authorities, ancient and modern: the other is that by recognising Poetry as—in the manner I have endeavoured to describe—the true carrying out and efflorescence of a human soul, according *to its own laws*, this theory assigns to Poetry its due position among the Works of that Creator Who, by what we call secondary causes and effects, evolves the graduated succession of relations, and by the harmony of each with each insures the unison of each with all—suns with far solar centres, worlds with suns, inhabitants with worlds, trees with the

---

[1] See also Layamon's version as approaching in some of its details to Tennyson's.—J. N.

soil, leaves and blossoms with the tree, Man with his place, Man's works with man, and all things with Himself —and shows the perfect human Poem to be a word in the eternal utterance of the One Almighty Poet—a congruous passage in that Poem of the Universe which is the ordered expression of His Wisdom and His Love.

ILLUSTRATIVE NOTES ON POETRY AND ART.

WHY POETRY SHOULD BE RELIGIOUS, AS DISTINCT FROM METAPHYSICAL.

A TRUTH is not Religious unless its analogues, homologues, or other congruous types can be understood in all other great departments of Thought : *i.e.* unless it will form part of a congruous system that shall comprehend all the chief interests of Mankind.

Whatever mode of thinking is necessarily confined to one or two points of the mental compass may be true but is not Religious.

Whatever form of a truth is incongruous with *anything* insuperable in the constitution or action of the human mind is not a Religious form.

Poetry therefore should be always Religious as distinct from Metaphysical. Because the Religious statement of Truth is such a version of it in any one department as can be congruously carried out into all others without anywhere being inconsistent with the constitution of Man.

FOOT-NOTES FOR LECTURE.

Science (see Newton) says (as its fundamental axiom) we are to apply terrestrial principles to celestial phenomena—*i.e.* that the universe is one idea. Poetry acting on this is employed in showing the relations of its parts.

De Candolle tells us that a tree is a confederation of little trees. Human Physiology seems to indicate that the nervous system is an association of men, and the tendency of all science is to reduce phenomena to the varied application of one Principle.

A tree is a good illustration (remembering De Candolle's version of a tree) of the Law of a Poem, but the higher forms of creation are better, inasmuch as that is the finest work in which the greatest variety of application is consistent with unity in the Principle applied.

Language when analyzed is more than even a combination of words in literal senses.

Examine any passages of ordinary prose and you find that element by which the unseen is expressed—the metaphorical element. The Poets are the source of all this.

68   ARTISTIC.

Again the expressiveness of nouns, etc., of physical meaning is due to certain intimate relations between sign and thing signified. The Poets determine this.

Few words are used in *their central sense*: in innumerable cases an accidental sense having become the accepted meaning. Poets restore the central sense.

ILLUSTRATIONS OF PROSE AND POETRY.

Go through a series of events under the constraining conditions of ordinary life. Remember and recount them accurately in the acted series. Prose.

Now tell the same story with such differences as result from allowing the facts to perfect themselves individually and to follow the order of essential association. Poetry.

Take a specimen of faulty prose and subtract from it all that is inconsistent with the qualities of an ideal man— *e.g.* his Love, Worship, Knowledge—and with those things which those qualities necessitate in their expression—*e.g.* Beauty, Sublimity, Order—and the quotient, if any, will be Poetry—the zero of Poetry, may be.

As an illustration of the axiom that Poetry is what

will congruously form part of a Poem take the Scriptural passages adapted into Milton's seventh Book.

Contemplate a thing with all your powers—intellectual and moral—at once, and find a word or phrase that is the algebraic expression of that combination of forces and you speak Poetry, which is good in proportion to the degree in which your mind—at that time—is perfect.

NECESSITY OF RHYTHM.

The unity of Law which has been shown to be essential to a Poem is as essential to the whole body of sound in which the inaudible materials are incorporated as to those materials. The total sound in the Poem may be taken as a great organized corpus.

Now whether we consider sound, *per se*, as an unorganized thing to be measured by quantity, or as a succession of impulses to the ear, or of efforts by the organs of speech, and therefore as consisting of numbers, the first necessity of reducing it to proportion must be a standard unit of measure. This being fixed a subordination of parts to the Law of a whole becomes possible.

Hence feet and metre: and rhythm which is a composition of the standard of measure whereby the standard itself is nevertheless suggested by the proportions borne to it.

ARTISTIC.

Rhythmus—rest and action occurring at intervals either pre-expected or self-justificatory by perceptible relation to the previous intervals.

All co-operative movements of many things that are obliged to conform to one time-beater, like the heart, must be rhythmic in order to avoid collision.

As a piece of Art how fine are those two verses—the last of John vii. ('and every man went unto his own house') and the first of John viii. ('Jesus went unto the Mount of Olives')—in which, out of the dispersion and confusion of the scene, the principal Figure comes into principality by the size and dignity of 'Mount of Olives' as compared with 'own house.'

METAPHOR.

A great part of the Poet's work is the making of equations. He finds 'A' to be the equivalent of 'B' —i.e. 'A' being presented to his balanced mind would induce the same change therein as the presentation of 'B.' Metaphor in a true Poet is not a work of conscious human intellect at all: it is the perfunctory work of a piece of Divine machinery which produces the *alter ego* of a fact involuntarily. A Poet therefore must describe what he sees in Imagination (whether the images there be simply remembered or also reconstructed) for the Emotions produced in his mind by positive *Things* would usually be so exquisite as to make any verbal equivalent impossible.

Nevertheless the verbal equivalents which he finds for Memories and Imaginations appear to the rest of mankind equivalents for Things. We understand therefore how much beyond the ordinary race are the perceptions of the Poet and comprehend Tennyson's

> 'Dower'd with the hate of hate, the scorn of scorn,
> The love of love.'

CONSTRUCTION.

Every grown up full-functioned Human Being comes, more or less theoretically, to believe in an outside world of what he calls things, or facts, and an inner world which he calls himself.

Things in himself which he calls wishes or desires make him attempt to change the *status quo* of external things: to bring those together which were apart and separate those which were together. In this attempt he finds certain hindrances from 'properties' or conditions of outward and inward things; and finds that realization of his wishes is possible only by a selective compliance with these 'properties' and that execution of the attempt becomes easy in proportion as he conforms to the necessities these impose.

He whose activities have so wisely complied as to change the manner in which any set of 'external' things stand to each other has produced a ποίημα—his doing is ποίησις and himself a ποιητής.

ART AN INSTRUMENT OF PROGRESS.

A Logician, *per specialité*, can seldom be a good (and is always a dangerous) man of action, because he will absolutely deduce from premises which, since perceived by imperfect men, are, by necessity, partly false.

Other men may 'happen' upon a felicitous entirety of temporary right, but he, in some part of his work, and often in the whole, *must* be consistently and inevitably wrong.

The harmony and consistency of every organism that is to live and act—whether political or otherwise—must not be that of Logic but of Art.

The great progress of things takes place by the passage of the highest *form* of each thing into the thing above it.

Art should be an instrument of this progress by

always selecting the best phase of every individual, the best form of every type—*i.e.* the Ideal.

A WORK OF ART NEVER STRICTLY TELEOLOGIC.

That work of Art which in construction is strictly teleologic—in which every part is essential to the whole—is artificial not natural, architecture not Nature.

A work of Art should be a part—a membrum—of the great *Corpus Naturæ*; a whole in so far as a member is a whole *quoad* itself, but containing many things which are not essential to that whole insomuch as they have relation to the greater whole whereof it is a part.

By omitting those things, in the attempt at a theoretical completeness, the work falls from Art to mechanics. Hence the lifelessness and undivineness of much that is called Art.

(The sculptor knows that he can destroy the life of the most lovely marble face by simply making its two sides geometrically equal.)

HIGH ART NOT LITERAL.

As an unliving thing. absolutely still—having not one of the infinitesimal motions that are incessant in the living surface—would, if an exact form-and-colour likeness of life, produce, in a few minutes in the beholder, an instinctive horror, may it not be a primary condition of all 'ocular' Art that it shall demonstrate its non-reality by some radical 'manque?' That colour should not have substance, or substance colour?

Art, though it cannot hope to produce Truth, is an aspiration and effort towards Truth, and must therefore be essentially uncongenial with lying.

Is not the lie of the marble Venus, with skin of exquisite colour and all that should result from a *substance* of organic life, but whose interior is a dead mass of inorganic stone, a greater lie than the almost nothing of canvas?

IN WHAT MANNER ART SHOULD RE-PRESENT NATURE.

There are a thousand primroses on yonder Bank. What do I want Art to do for me? To reproduce the Bank as it is? That may be worth doing if practicable, but, for my part, I would rather wait the next Spring and see the Bank itself at the right season.

What I want Art to do is to bring a mind specially gifted to perceive among that thousand of Primroses the most typical Primrose—the αὐτὸ καθαυτόν—and to perpetuate *that* for me, so that looking at any time on that special Perfection I may not only receive the accompanying enjoyment but rise towards Perfection Universal.

ART SHOULD TAKE POSSESSION OF MENTAL HABITS.

In Art we should take possession of mental habits, inveterate ideas, invariable experiences, and natural functions: *e.g.* when Domenichino makes the nymph's foot look elastic the *unconscious* logic of the mind supplies motion: when the Apollo Belvedere is seen at that infinitesimal point of rest which must intervene in steps, the same logic takes the step: &c. &c.

MEMORY.

It is probable that human Memory, in all cases, follows, with more or less ability, the laws of Poetic Imagination—omitting and rearranging according to Unity.

We see this on the large scale in the National Memory wherein facts become congruous and beautiful. I am not now alluding to the grotesque elements in Mythology which are due to another process.

SKETCHES FROM NATURE.

THE WORLD IN EARLY SUMMER.

Who *sees* and feels it? A few poets.

Are the rest of mankind unmoved? No; but how much? As much as by food or wine? No. In the next ages it shall be as delightful to them as a dinner. In ages after as friendship, heroic war, manly exercise, a good action. In ages after as the rarest ecstasy of Devotion or of Love.

Our savage ancestors and the classic masters of the world saw the same Nature that meets our eyes. The sky and clouds were the same. The trees no higher, and in spring and autumn their leaves came and went with the same colours and the same miracle of perfection. And, however rude the walls they built, ferns, ivies, mosses, and leaning traceries beautified them as exquisitely as now. They lived among a prophecy of more ideal generations.

APRÈS? (MEMORANDUM FOR A LITTLE POEM.)

Thou that delightest in Spring—that feelest what is the Primrose—the Summer can bring thee nothing. Thou foreknowest all it can give and art not moved.

Yet still this delight?

Therefore thou must be created to delight in it.

What then—art thou part of all? or Whom dost thou, ignorant, acknowledge?

Or is it but the memory of that early time when Hope promised everything in every year? And Hope like Love hath brightest visions just before he waketh. Hath he not yet quite awakened and dreams the dream of youth?

BELLS AT NIGHT.

If without human agency such a sound undulated out of the earth what inferences of life and soul should we draw! Yet a more exquisite music is always making thereby which we hear with the eye.

I perceive in the organs of the senses, from touch up to and including sight, but various modes of *hearing*—the eye being the most exquisite ear.

The true eye has yet to be opened.

SPRING.

The springness of a very early spring-evening, while as yet the earth is unchanged, as if spring odours could be discerned by the eye.

(In spring-twilight.) Soft, palpitating, crepuscular,—as if the shadows of the leaves to come were flickering in the air.

The first green on the trees—like a green haze, or cloud, self-sustained.

The opening of the Hawthorns—like a slow dawn in the Moon that takes a week of earthly days.

Effect of extreme quiet on a spring evening. The trees so still that the air between them seems to move. What was mere space and division becomes the active world and the substantial subsides into the demarcations that divide a world of spirits.

The Spring Orchards—As though the children of the year, in masquerade, played at their parents: and one was Grandsire Winter with his snows; another Dawn; the starry Meadows Night: but, by the family likeness, all so transposed and transfused that Night was a very

Day, Winter a miracle of Summer, and Dawn half hidden in the golden hair of that Noon on whom she leaned.

While on the melting sense, above, around,
Warm, green, and golden, through the trembling air
Spring, like a dropping splendour of the Morn,
Silent as gums and odours, slow distilled
From the embowering trees.

SUNSET, DAWN, ETC.

After sunset in June—the sky from North-East to South-West like a harvest-kingdom of red wheat.

Dawn—In a cloudless dawn over the sea a red (from deep-red to rose-red and then to red-golden) and golden glory twenty degrees wide and in the midst of the rose-red of it the Morning star.

Summer Lightning at Night—Rosy, like sudden Dawns. Sometimes iridescent, like the iridescence of hot metal.

THE MORNING STAR.

Full of day,
And through the stellar people of the night

walking like one awake
Amid a world of sleepers.

THE EVENING STAR.

And as an eye moistened by some sweet thought
Glistens, dissolves its light, and overfills,
And drops a tear and shines,
And, by this rise and fall exstils
The lustrous April of its smiling grief.—

THE MOON.

Some warm cloud immaculate
Doth take the cold moon, which more white or less,
(As virtue in a vestal and a bride
Wears here or here the sweet comparative,
As we conceive of Virtue)
Lies in the hand of morning like a pearl
And by dead beauty doth secern and mark
The supersubtle difference, which, being Life,
Is all Divine.

THE WINTER MOON.

The waning white of a disastrous moon
On ghastly snows and haggard in the sea.

NUCLEI.

A Bunch of field-flowers—May 22,—*Varieties of green.* Delicate green of new fern, shadowed by creases on each side the chief vein of the *pinna* (creases as by the touch of an elastic finger in clay) and by the down-curling of the *pinnæ* themselves, and by the incipient seeds on their undersides.

Misty green of the upside, and grey of the downside of the new and veined leaf of the service tree : one side of each *sulcus* shadowed when the upside of the leaf faces the sun, and the veins looking dark when seen from beneath in that position, but when the underside faces the sun the veins shining, transparent, a golden green. The stem grey with fairy fogs of down.

Spurge, carrying golden crescents, a little ball of sovereignty and two bells—as it were insignia—in bronze salvers.

Red campion with its purple green, as if the blood of the *flower* shone in passing through it upwards.

The yellowish green of the yellow wood nettle—as if refraction from that fire the flower.

The strong tenderness and rough softness of the fresh-grown shoot of the hazel-nut—with its yellow-green leaf browned with a nutty promise of sun and weather.

The Solomon-seal leaf, with its many silver veins, a mere coloured net to catch light, which one sees alive within its exquisite meshes,—the whole now greener, now brighter, as the white captive moves or is quiet. And the flower-bud where the colour of the green stem seems to have trickled down the ivory and to hang at the top ready to fall in a green drop.

And the sweet-brier from which, as from a key-note, all the others make their 'differences.'

And the young shoot of the yew—

> As if the woody heart of some brown oak
> —Like a stern ancient that, unapt to change,
> Looks with another Nature on the young,
> Yet in a fine decorum, with no joy,
> Fits to his time, and takes the passing mode
> Of the new world—had fallen at season due
> Into a leafy fashion.

The Bramble—in his innocent complexion—

> That like the infant Martyr of the tale
> Bears now the fated blood that he must shed
> In purple Autumn.

The Oak—born old, that but in manhood green,
Comes from the womb the presage of that self
Whose yellow front shall stay the ravenous face

Of hollow winter, and with threatening arms
And flattering gold cover the shrieking flight
Of the dishevelled year.

In a night journey June 14, observed the following symptoms of the dissolution of Night in the following order :—

I. The vegetation on the banks of pools was reflected—not in colours but in shadowy somewhats—in the water.

II. The tufts of grass or weeds in fields were visible as tufts, by being lighter on one side than the other—or rather lighter *above* than *below*.

III. The willows were perceptible as willows (being silvery-leafed.)

IV. Vegetation grew green.

V. Mists began to rise from all waters and waste places. I. and II. were noticeable before any notable change had taken place in the apparent darkness of the air.

Nature provides two climacterics—one of flowers for the soul, one of fruits for the body ; and each interdependant like soul and body.

A nosegay should be as if what perfect order had arranged a wind of variety had touched into lovely discomposure.

Mountain Paths that lead where?
Into the Spring, into the Morning, into young Love, into old Memory—wherever one may enter into pure beauty and colour as a bee into a flower.

A Royal Scion—the autocracy of a thousand years looked out of him in unutterable pathos. The race had learned 'vanity of vanities' though the individual was still in the excitement and joy of youthful hope.

In sudden rain after great sunshine the leaves of sycamore and beech lift their sides so as to produce a temporary cup to catch it.

In ploughed or broken-up fields, without turf but waste, daisies have a larger stem than ordinary, to lift the flower above the knobs of mould.

When a mist comes up the glen, the insects flee before and on each side—and the swallows. These fugitives devour each other. The analogue of an invading army and contending civil factions.

At Sunset.—The shadows of the breakers in the wet sand. The manifold motions, simultaneous and not incongruous, the roll of the tide, the diagonal of the ripple, the transverse of the footsteps of the wind.

———

An old unsatisfactory existence.

As in a showery summer the dull brown overcast covers all the sky. But rains fall, and along the summit of the hills the blue empty sky appears, like a pause in great Music, and tears clear the whole vacant heaven—

And, lo, above the hill-tops, white and slow,
Immaculate, unhasting, undelayed,
In form an Alp, ...
. . . a great cloud majestical
Into the unpossessed and favouring Heaven
Rises to occupation, like the grand
New Life.

———

The Dawn,
Like a celestial countenance, made holy
By an Almighty Knowledge of sweet Things,
Looks in its calm content of happy promise
   Upon the advancing Earth.

As when the Dawn
Glows o'er the glowing Deep, and sea and sky
Are but asunder as a two-leaved book,
All of one story, and the Ocean-Heaven
And Heavenly Ocean seem as when at first,
Like a ripe fruit, in twain did God divide
The waters from the waters.

. . . . As when the wave that drowns a ship,
And callous as a sexton's hand, lets down
The mighty coffin, and heaves on its way
Shoreward, and coming is long seen far off,
   Darker than Death, remorseless as the Grave,
   Mounting and falling—
And from its pitiless bulk of rolling gloom
The sudden axe of some avenging rock,
   Hews out a passionate heart, whiter than snow,
   And tenderer than the lilies.

The innumerable roar
Of that one multiform sea, that all life long
Divides the time with thunders.

Men who plough the sea,
And feed the sinewy might of knotted limbs
Upon its toilsome harvests.

To the wide serene
Of whose uncut existence, this our world,
And all its peopled water-drop of air,
And all our fretful pulse of night and day,
Marked nothing—   .   .   .   .
.   .   .   .   As when
The fairy eft that thro' Italian boscage
Darts his small lightning of thin shade from bosc
To bosc, or stopping midway shows a heart
Swift as the buzzing flitter of a fly,
Doubtless a heart, but yet to us with hearts
No heart that can be lived by, yet no less
To the poor petty tenant of the dust,
The rhythm of being and the clock of life.

COLOUR. (CANNES.)

· Illustration of congruity in Natural Phenomena, due to essential causes.

All the colours of the sea and of fish: which can only be expressed one by the other.

The colours of insects and vegetation : only to be expressed one by the other.

After hours of intense light cover your eyes with a white bandage. You will see a species of green, a species of 'lake' (madder lilac), and a species of blue.

Open your eyes and look. You will find this green under the wings of this Cleopatra butterfly : pull open, for the first time, the great nozzle of that Aloe, you will find it within. You will see it, less exquisitely the same, in all the corn of the South, and in the leaves of many plants.

You will find that 'lake' tinting the tenderest edges of the young vine leaves and shoots, those of the oak, and of other unfolding trees and plants, and in every dilution see it in the anemones, the peach-orchards, the edges of clouds, the evening sky.

You will find the blue in the flax blossom in this field; it bears the same relation to primitive blue that this green and 'lake' bear to green and red.

The *difference* puts them in relation with the grey of the Olive, the colour of whose fruit is the lake condensed, and whose youngest leaves show *the green*.

Observe those Olives against the south-eastern sky in winter just after sunset, when the under-sides of their leaves are turned up and visible and lose themselves in the identical grey of the lower sky, which passes higher up into dove-colour. Bring down your eyes and find this unspeakable dove-colour in the palm-leaves and observe that they bear the relation to yellow which the green, lake, and flax-blue bore to their bases.

The anemone that is of the 'lake' described, is nearest in colour to lilac or musk geranium.

EVENING AT SAN REMO.

The Sun being lower than the promontories, the sea smooth ; a blue evening is in the bay, having a sharp line of limit from promontory to promontory.

Between this line and an horizon of purple, upper-edged with crimson-amber, the sea one pearl, one welfare, as might be the seas of Heaven, where milky light not yet fired into immateriality lay in an ocean of potential Good, ready to lave and nourish, or to bear the happy ships (with sails of live gold) without effort of their own or upper wind.

Indeed the unshaped substance of a possible universe of bliss, only as yet showing its ἐνέργεια by that action.

JANUARY 17th. (AT SAN REMO.)

In the midst of eastern clear Heaven, over the Mediterranean, a heavy island of snow cloud, black with substance and livid with cold, touching the sea sometimes by great roots (with intervals), sometimes by a rolling smoke, as of battle, and leadening it into the deadly coma of the weaker possessed by the stronger.

The Sea (at San Remo) in undulating calms. The nautili and pearl, and every tinted secret of inner shells, and every shelly phantasy of million-minded colour, existing beforehand in solution.

In great heat the leaves of the Olive rise till the points are nearly vertical. At this time if the wind is opposite the sun a brilliant shimmer as of diamonds (without iridescence) or of dew. If the wind is with the sun, or in calm, the special grey.

Moonlight in the Bay of Naples. Half-past three A.M. April 10, 1865.

The line of mountains on Sorrento-shore visible to the end.

Full moon setting west.

In the sky overhead a rose and consciousness, and a sense like the remembrance of exquisite greenery, but no hint of sunrise or of eastward-dawn.

Westward, towards moon-set, a warmer light than moonlight—like a feminine reflection of sunset-afterglow—

>As though dreaming Dian
>Through the white virgin of her maiden sleep
>Takes the forbidden sweet.

SPECULATIVE

SPECULATIVE.

LIKE Zaccheus small of stature I make this Igdrazil of the Universe the Sycamore whereinto I climb to see Christ.

[N. B. As in all other instances, the passages collected under this heading are memoranda made in different note-books, and at very different dates, now first brought together. It is thought better on the whole that slight inconsistencies and occasional repetitions should occur rather than that any effort should be made to recast the original matter into more finished form: but with regard to these passages more than to any other part of the volume, it is felt important that the reader should be requested to bear in mind the manner in which they were found—as Fragments, the intention of which could only have been fully understood had the writer been able to carry out the Design which, fitting them into their destined places, would have shown their proportionate relation as parts to a whole.—ED.]

SEARCH FOR THE IDEAL.

IN thinking of Truth it is to be borne in mind that we have nothing to do with things as *they are*, but with Things as they would appear to a perfect and perfectly healthy human Being.

This is Truth : and it may happen therefore that a nearer knowledge of the absolute nature of things may be a deviation from the Truth, so far as we are concerned, because different from that knowledge of them which the Creator has assigned to an ideal Humanity.

Philosophy is not a statement of things as they are, but a physiological biography of the human soul under the exciting causes of the Universe. Its results merely give us the present physiology, morphology, and dynamics of the soul.

Suppose man to be instead of the creation of a Superior, the better result of a process of an inferior—a spirit evolved in the substance of fermenting matter,—a product of growth.

But this presupposes an enormous *petitio principii*. We have no proof that growth itself, or any material evolution of the better from the worse, could take place in the absence of a still Higher Perfection; that any movement of the grosser towards the fine would be possible, but that gross and fine are alike held in solution by a still subtler and finer—the Alkahest of God.

Granted that to determine the existence of an Ideal is difficult. But there are other things equally difficult to identify, which, nevertheless, no one scruples to erect as standards :—*Health*, for instance.

There is a tendency in all things—in the whole Cosmos and in its individual constituents—to struggle towards health. *Hope*, in the soul, seems the unconscious witness of this principle of things.

It is to the necessity, arising from the constitution of the Human Mind, for an Ideal of Humanity, that we owe those resemblances in Mythology to the Ideal Man

Christ, which have been misunderstood to be traditionally derived.

Anaxagoras and Protagoras arrived at false conclusions, because when laying down that 'whatever seems is true,' they left out the conditioning clause—' to the Ideal Man.'

The Ideal standard (of the Ideal Man) is more than ever (artistically) necessary, now that microscopes and photography are vitiating the consistency of human perceptions.

In the Ideal Human Being—Image of God—the Human Differentia is no longer in quality but in quantity, and in him therefore takes place the καταλλαγή —atonement, as Shakspeare always uses the word or its derivatives—of the Race.

The Ideal is not a mere algebraic power of the Imperfect. There is an Embryology of the moral Nature. Examine the Embryology of the physical in animal and vegetable; show how the phases of development are *not* miniatures of the ultimate phase: that in some cases the progress *appears* deviation. Apply this to mental developments, where a simulacrum of the ultimate perfection is not so near it as apparent variation, *e.g.* the premature destruction of human feeling—as in monastic and fakir discipline—further from the mental cosmos of Perfection than the exuberance of unsubordinated emotions: *e.g.* (also) the despotism of husband over wife, nearer to the ideal of union than the crude equality of ordinary modern theorists.

If this earth were inhabited by perfect bodies and perfect souls its evils would be at zero.

It is for Science to superintend the attainment of one desideratum, and Religion of the other.

The Kingdom of Heaven may be so much of Earth as is making itself Divine, as distinguished from the rest.

The truth as to Ideals was perceived separately in two halves by Greek and Christian. The Greek saw in the world and the body the possibilities of ideal perfection, and sought to realize it in Art by combining its elements.

The Christian saw only the imperfection, and seeing this, without also seeing the relation to the perfect, and the perfectibility implied in that, looked upon it as Satanic.

In result the Greek, unable to personalize the true perfect, made Gods of imperfection ; the Christian made demons of destinies that should have developed to Power.

Both were right and wrong; we are in once Gods and devils.

Liberalism is over controls and becomes individual judgment, by saying if your thought is inconsistent with a principle laid down by the best minds in that department it is wrong, or if consistent you are justified in your speculation.

"To do one's best."—a good illustration of principles deducted from law. The principle of true moral existence being to discern right and wrong, and whatever garnishes, impedes, or distorts the true power of good qualities.

The object of the philanthropist should be a scene of things where no one could rise up to a grey day and a godless world.

 See Mill.—Limitations to Liberty.—J. N.

COMPARATIVE IDEOLOGY.

In considering the sources of all ideas we have

A. The physical world, not human, but with a *potential humanity*.

B. The mental world, not physical, but with a *potential physics*.

The interaction of B with A has this among other modes: some portion of B embodies itself in some portion of A—attracted thereto not by the *whole* of that portion of A, but by the special affinities in that portion. But once embodied it remains as that whole portion, the non-affinities of the portion included. This resultant B × A is again received by B as objective knowledge. More of the potential humanities in the A of this B × A are assimilated by B than those which were the original special affinities, and the given B that originally embodied itself in the given A, is now increased by the addition of these new extractions. Thus increased it once more seeks embodiment in an ampler portion of A (the former having become effete in the same way that a metaphor becomes at length literal and is then disused for other figures), which in turn goes through the same process.[1]

[1] See Hegel and Malthus on the evolution of mind from matter. —J. N.

The testimony to an Ideal can be inferred by all of us from the fact that of things of the same kind we approve individuals more or less, and by admitting a better imply the possibility of a Best.

This Best it would be easy to discover if we were all of one mind. But our differing powers produce different judgments. All search for an ideal, therefore, prenecessitates the search for an ideal percipient—an ideal Man.

Again we may say an ideal thing is that which best fulfils its Law, is in the most perfect grammatical construction.

But if reason be the grammar of that construction, we require first to find and apply the grammar. And man is the highest reason which we humanly can investigate or apply, and a perfect Man the highest form of that highest Reason.

If there existed but one specimen of each type, no notion of an ideal would be suggested. In speaking of a Better, we mean either one more suited to certain wants in us (which 'Better' does not suggest an Ideal), or one more truly realizing a Design or Pattern perceptible in each imperfect specimen. By observing many imperfect specimens—*e.g.* of an animal—the nature of the bones, muscles, &c., more or less eminent in them suggests the object the animal is to effect. But this suggestion does not furnish the Ideal, for Nature is never finitely teleologic.

But by crossing a specimen by another wherein the deficiencies of each are compensated, a progeny results wherein Nature in her own way—(*i.e.* with many other accomplishments included) remedies those defects. And by a repetition of this process a being results by whom the recognized object is *perfectly* effected.

But this Being will contain many qualities, as Beauty and variety of function, which could not have been foreseen by a study of the imperfect specimen. An ideal therefore cannot be theoretically arrived at, it must be found in existence, and the existence of such Ideals might be reasoned, *à priori*, either on ancient or modern principles.

Now if Science wishes by dissection or examination of a specimen to understand the laws of any Being, she would choose one of these perfect examples—sure that in such she shall find the fulfilment and rationale of functions and facts that in the imperfect were incomplete and perplexing.

Since the Perfect and imperfect specimen differ not

radically but in degree it must be always unsafe to reason from the phenomena of the Imperfect, because we have no guarantee that in such a specimen any given phenomenon is truly accounted for. Whatever is fragmentary —*i.e.* is separated from its co-ordinates—must, if it is organic, contain facts that exist in relation to others not contained in the specimen—causes without effects, *e.g.* desire without fruition,—and what under other conditions we should term effects appearing without their explanatory antecedents—*e.g.* a beautiful eye but no optic nerve. (The cruder *species* of vegetable genera offer illustrations of the same truth.)

This which applies to all organized Beings applies pre-eminently to Man.

The principles of Humanity, or the rationale of Human functions, must therefore be investigated in the Perfect Man—the Human Being as he would be if all his powers and functions were arrived at that positive and relative state, that singular quality and quantity, and that proportional combination, wherein, most favourably to the welfare of the parts and of the whole, they could realize a composite existence and activity. Such a Being, passive and active, is the standard of everything Human. He is the living Law, the concrete Logos, the pure Human Good.

TO FIND THE IDEAL MAN.

We have all some qualities common to the Perfect Man, which, by the sensations they give us, testify of themselves (*i.e.* secure an involuntary respect from our *ego*) and by other external facts get their testimony ratified, as being 'better' than the rest. The lowest human being is, therefore, a sufficient basis for the operation of search. But during many stages of the process, after leaving that first starting-point, we shall seem little nearer to our end—nay often retrograding, but the sum of all the zigzags will be an upward movement, and when they are once surmounted the way is easy and direct.

Process. Ask your lowest human being whom he considers a model man. Ask the same question of his model and so forwards.

The difficulty at first will arise from the large admixture of other than ideal qualities in the given models, and the certainty that some one in the series may refer you to another his superior *only* in the lower attributes ; but the general law will vindicate itself in the long run, and by sufficient patience in tracing from link to link the chain will again slant upwards.

As you reach the nobler types the experiment more

rapidly culminates and with but one result. Wherever tried, in whatever age and country, there is one sentence which is the shorthand of all the verdicts of the World—

'In the image of God made He man.'

RELATION OF IMPERFECT TO IDEAL ACTION AND EXPRESSION.

The Ideal Man must not only exist but express his existence.

He does this by γνῶσις, and by ποίησις—whether of gesture, action, poems, painting, architecture, etc.

Poetry therefore comprehends nearly the whole expression of a perfect human Being, ... but it may be asked, if Poetry be the language of a perfect World—(speech as it would spontaneously exist among perfect human beings) of what value to imperfect Humanity could be the discovery of its nature.

The too-ready answer of some idealists would be that it is the whole duty of the imperfect humanity to copy the actions of the Perfect. But since in an imitation of this kind action would cease to be *expression*, and, therefore, would cease to be truth, such ὑπόκρισις whether in the moral or intellectual functions is alike destructive.

The true answer implies a principle of curious

importance which I hope at some other time to illustrate more at large — the principle of mental embryology.

It is ascertained that in the prenatal development of organized bodies the phases of the fœtus, instead of being a gradual epiphany of the final shape, are forms of types of being utterly different in powers and functions from that which the embryon is nevertheless steadily approaching.

The development of the human character exhibits a similar law, and is often nearer to its final type when apparently diverse from it than when exhibiting the appearance of similitude.

But there is something *quoad* which the outward signs of the imperfect man may, without untruth to himself, be ruled by those of the perfect. It is the qualities which they express: *e.g.* the quality of Love, little or great, of Justice, little or great, &c., &c.

That is absolutely—*quoad hominem*—right or wrong, which would be done or lived by the Ideal Man under the given circumstances—a system of perfect morality therefore would be merely a chronicle of his spontaneities.

But for the *imperfect* humanity to do or say what would be the true expression of the *perfect* would be false, a systematized hypocrisy : *e.g.* to say for his little love, little gratitude, little perception, the words which were the exact impersonation of the great : and so of all deeds,—which are but language.

True morality, therefore, is a system of principles— the formulæ of those qualities which under every variation of circumstances would move the perfect man; qualities to become action according to the *status* of the agent.

Duty therefore, in any given case, is the existence of that *quality* which would act in the perfect man, and that *expression* thereof which is *true* to the then *status* of the agent. This applies to men in their corporate as well as individual capacity.

Therefore Christianity cannot work without human nature, nor human nature without Christianity. Christianity supplies the Principles, the human being is the measure of their application. The two together being a perfect system, and, when so united, throughout Divine. The constitution of each man determines his vocation, Christianity furnishes the principles of all vocations, the two together constitute the autonomy of the individual. In other words a perfect principle applied to the best of an imperfect ability.

These principles can only be learned in the person of

an absolutely *perfect Man* because in any lower grade of progress some of them exist in an embryonic form which either appears to be antagonistic to the final or is superfluous to it.

In illustration of foregoing—suppose a man bursting with reverent gratitude throws himself on his face. But suppose a man with little gratitude or reverence to do the same.

Is the posture of the body acceptable to God?

But it may be objected that, by the congruities of nature, a given bodily posture is likely to stimulate a given mental attitude, and that he who kneels being irreverent may gradually become reverent.

It may be true that some small spiritual effect may take place through the external pose, and it may be also true that a general course of hypocrisy may involuntarily induce an inner change for the better, but the fact remains the same that a more truthful expression of devotion, under the existing state of feeling, would be still more certain to culture that feeling into strength, and that the unmistakeable evils of hypocrisy are greater than its concealed and questionable good.

It is not enough, under given circumstances, to show that a benefit takes place. You require to show that it is the greatest possible under them.

The soul must act—the soul's action is alone true action—and the soul's action must take that bodily action which is congruous with it, and no other.

The foregoing notions of Duty are not inconsistent with the doctrine of obedience. The obedience required by God is the *soul's* obedience. Bodily obedience takes its nature from the nature of the simultaneous spiritual action: *e.g.* to give alms to him one hates is not charity; it may be piety and self-sacrifice. To abstain from her one lusts after is not purity: and so of other examples— *e.g.* 'though I give all my goods to feed the poor and have not *charity*—'

A pious man, therefore, may do the deeds of all the virtues—not, however, exactly *as* the virtuous do them— without possessing any virtue but one. His value (in relation to other virtuous men) must depend on whatever proportion the value of so much of this one virtue may bear to the accumulated value of the absent virtues. And this sum no mortal judge can do.

But I think the sound procedure for a pious man deficient in the other virtues is not to perform the *acts* of those virtues on the scale, or in the manner of the perfect man, but to stimulate the germs of these virtues within him and let their acts follow the law I have previously suggested.

'*Be* ye perfect.' Not *seem* ye.

As regards Duty it is probable that each increase of a beautiful function is accompanied with a reaction on the intellect (imagination) by which is created a higher notion of the possible exercise of the functions than its then powers can spontaneously realize, and that, therefore, a duty-standard on sliding scale may never cease.

I think, however, that such artificial function can only be requisite till the congenial co-operation of *all* mental functions is attained: after which exercise would be the sole education.

For textual support of this theory of duty, &c., see Luke vi. 40, 'The disciple is not above his master : but everyone that is perfect shall be as his master.'

Now this formula of Duty applies as much to the intellectual as the moral province.

The Principles of Perfect Human Speech given, in varying application, to all human speech whatever, and those Principles, which applied by the imperfect Being result in a prose that more or less expresses his imperfection, applied by the Perfect have their produce in Poetry.

BEAUTY, LOVE, ORDER, UNITY.

MANY psychical things—*e.g.* feelings—can only be understood by ascertaining the attributes of their ideal or perfect state.

Beauty is that which is loved to delight (by the Ideal Man). Beauty is the *harmony* of rhythmic *parts*. Is not Beauty visible Love?

Love is an effort of the soul towards unity; the oscillation of the soul between the desire for identity and the necessity for difference; that broad affection of the Mind (or of a mental function) which has its apex and climax in Delight (or any motion of the soul in that series whose top and climax is Delight). It begins in choice. Therefore, as from the ephemera we go back stage by stage and find the same being under different forms, as from the flower we trace backwards to the germen, as from the crisis of disease we see phase by phase along its unity to a comparatively inert incipience, so we would identify as

Love whatever by natural order can intensify and culminate into Delight, however little like that ultimate efflorescence its given state may appear.

The first motions of Life show a power of choice—to attract and repel—to attract the congruous and repel the incongruous—to bring sameness of essence into sameness of place. (Congruous—*i.e.* that which has potential unity. In the action of living matter this congruity is between matter and matter. Matter attracts to itself that which is capable of unification; the nature of the activity—the *vis*—by which the attraction is made is inappreciable by us. So far vegetation. In the first examples of higher life we have evident *choice* directing the attraction. An instinct for 'sameness' exists in forms of life too crude to allow of comparison or conscious intelligence.)

Tracing this attraction and repulsion upward we find it rising in the higher animals to what we call love and disgust.

Love is the form in higher grades of life of that which in lower grades is shown by choice, which *attracts the congruous*: therefore the primary principles of Love being unity and order that which excites it must have unity and order. Love will then make it part of a new order and unity.

The primary principles of Beauty are, therefore, order and unity. But it is not enough for Beauty that it embody the primary principles. Human Love acts through material functions. As these are finite they cannot *persist*: as feeble they are unfit for violent change. The material in which Beauty exists has many modes of hurting them.

But when an object, having order and unity, has a variety that needs no persistence and a graduation of change that can be perceived without violent action, when, besides, it is free from any of those attributes of matter which hurt the sensorium, that sum-total excites the entire unobstructed unsubtracted perfection of Love—Delight—and is Beauty.

Love is—1. Accompanied with a tendency to fusion—as in friendship and some other passions.

2. Accompanied by the tendency to comprehend—as in the love of man for woman.

3. Accompanied by the tendency to be comprehended—as in the love of woman for Man, and of Man for God.

No. 2 responds to the Beautiful.

No. 3 responds to the Sublime.

Sorrow is Love No. 2 under conditions unfavourable to satisfaction. (It includes compassion or pity.)

Terror is Love No. 3 under such conditions.

The Love of Woman to Man is (similar to) the love of Man to God.

The Love of Man to Woman the Love of God to Man.

The fact that one is a perfect specimen of its type and the other for ever and necessarily an imperfect perhaps gives equality to the two.

Anger is a passion of immature Love, excited by contact with what is not beauty. When Love is full-grown and affixed this passion ceases—non-Beauty being merely ignored—but while immature it is necessary to its growth, as an elastic force to clear away unfavourable conditions.

The sensuous element of Love provides for such a general value of the body as is necessary to keep the other faculties from their native tendency to forsake it—(and, in pursuance thereof, to despise, ill-use, and degrade it).

That element cannot be absent without a consequent loss of equilibrium among the general scheme of faculties.

(*e.g.* the various extremes of eastern and western asceticism.)

On the other hand its presence, in the most refined, idealized, and exquisite form—a form in which it can hardly be recognized as of the same genus with the lower manifestations—is all that is necessary for this provision.

Love, the passion towards unity, is a direct agitation in the thing seeking unity, and differs, therefore, in its diagnosis as the thing differs.

A dull tendency, a furious appetite, a mild yearning, a strong ache, a grasping joy, a steady-burning happiness, a climacteric delight, and many other signs, being the Love-signs of these different substances, and existing in us simultaneously or consecutively as a different portion of the soul tends towards what seems good to it.

As in imperfect natures the tendencies of some of these 'different portions' may be inconsistent with others, the whole Love of that organic unity the total soul may require the sacrifice of some of those partitive 'loves,' or a substitution, in respect to them, of a tendency to union with the educational benefactor instead of the natural tendency of like to like, or apt to apt.

The union between apt and apt is the highest kind of

unity, because, while like and like united have (virtually in their different relations to space) a numeric difference, the new total of apt and apt united is a unity possible to neither separately, appertaining equally to both, and divisible by no defining lines.

The union of like and like though it produces a third thing, inasmuch as the whole is not the parts, has merely produced the fact of wholeness; while the union of apt and apt has not merely so done but has added a new creature besides.

ORDER.

Form is the condition of Phenomena: Order is the construction of them : Reason is the syntax of that construction.

To order is to make multiplicity into unity.

Order is the co-existence of things according to their mutual fitness : (*e.g.* ball and socket and their moral analogues.)

This *seems* to render the idea of the whole unnecessary, because it may be said that an infinite variety of forms exist, and that in an infinite succession of changes those cohere that can adhere.

As order is a co-existence of parts according to an overruling Law, the phenomenal exhibition of order requires a perceptible equivalent for that insensible Law.

It requires among co-existing parts a part of more dignity, or force, or size, as the bodily residence of that Law.

Suppose your Law is the Wrath of Achilles, the moment that Wrath is more than a formula it comes under the conditions of time and place, becomes incorporate, and must enter on relations with other bodies.

Again, as Order, in the abstract, is the regulation of many by One the concrete presentment of it must have the metaphors of these and of the intercourse between them. It may be that as the 'One' is the 'Law of the Whole,' and that as the whole consists of its parts, no 'one' can absolutely stand for the Law: but it can stand for it as much as phenomena ever do stand for forces. As much as what we call matter stands for motion. It cannot contain motion but it is our only and necessary means to an idea of it. And indeed what in a simple and mechanical manner is found to exist in crystallography may, in some more subtle fashion, exist in more complex combinations, and there may be a part in every structure which does truly concrete the Law of the Whole and wherefrom the Whole may be worked *ab intra*.

BEAUTY, LOVE, ORDER, UNITY.

Nor of origin—for where is *origin*? Nor a previous existence in unity; for to be in unity things must be related.

In that continual change of unity to multiplicity and multiplicity to unity which is in the process of things, are there not successional *gradus* and may not co-existence in a preceding *gradus* of unity be the test of relationship?

The various multiplicity of man co-existed in the phenomenal unity of the antεembryonic state. So that of the *tree* in the seed. This phenomenal unity was doubtless multiplicity but (to human senses) prephenomenal multiplicity.

The multiplicity therefore that has ever existed in this unity is capable of being composed into another kind of unity—is related. Germinal unity. Isospermism, or some similar name, should be given to that fact to which *relation* is due.

UNITY.

We arrive at Man in whom, among animals, Love takes its highest forms. Whether the soul be an undulation of the Infinite Oneness—a ripple that cannot return to the unity of the Sea—and having therefore the attraction of the stone towards the Mountain for the Unity out of which it came—we do not enquire, because we seek for practical knowledge : but we know that, among the primordial qualities of the Soul, the difference by which we first show that infinitude is lost is a desire towards unity. To choose, to like, to love—thus it desires (wrestling with the necessity to be individual) to end multiplicity by unity. But that desire must be intelligence to *know* the other and executive force to compose the two into unity.

To know things in that way which best helps to unity is to know their *essentials*.

When mentally we abstract qualities from anything till that quality which if abstracted would leave no difference between the thing and another thing, we have found its essential quality. Or, we may say, when substance, which *quoad our perceptions* is as nothing, begins to have qualities and to be something, there are primary '*qualities*' by which the something has separated itself from the nothing—*i.e.* the qualities and the quality which is nearest in order of phenomena to the nothing. Or, again, we may say, in those acts of intelligence by which we touch substance there are primary acts, *cardinal motions*, capable of certain variations within an autonomy.

But whatever be the soul it is so beset with matter

that it cannot move without causing material change; to cause change it must overcome inertia, change is the measure of expended force; if the soul had endless force it would be infinite, but it is finite, therefore its force is finite and can come to an end; but he who expends what can come to an end must needs husband. Therefore we may conclude there is a thrift in the self-preservation of the soul. If so, in using the material instrument it will spend no more force than needful to the fulfilment of desire; *i.e.* it will act with the least difference consistent with that *variety* which is necessary to the material function.

We find man with a soul that cannot be in direct contact with the outer world and which requires therefore a copy of that outer world—a representation—as the object of knowledge.

'To know' represents, then, a double action, of representation and cognizance. The conditions of his knowledge, therefore, are not only those of the perceiving but also of the representing function.

Whatever be 'to know'—whether

1st. The combined action of a mental function which merely mirrors—represents—the world, and a mental percipient that touches the representation, or

2nd. Whether the transmission of motion from the without to and through the within, or

3rd. Whether the reaction of a such and such force from within meeting and counteracting such and such a force from without, or

4th. Whether a change in, as it were, the shape of the soul, corresponding to the mould of external things—in any case knowledge in the perfect man has arrived at its best state. In any case it has the intervention of a 'material' machine, 'the body,' the possibilities of which condition for it the outer universe: *i.e.* the question of the nature of that universe becomes a question of the nature—*i.e.* the functional abilities—of that transmitting medium.

We find man in a body ruled by a heart that, in health, marks an exactly equal beat of time, and equally alternates rest and action, and the functions of which must, therefore, bear some proportionate relation to that time-keeper.

We find him acting by material functions—*e.g.* brain. Matter acting—*i.e.* moving—within limited space must move by oscillation—up and down or to and fro. If this oscillation is out of proportion to the proportions of those functions ruled by the heart, we should have obstruction and neutralization—lethargy or death. But we have total activity and life :—therefore the oscillation is continually proportionate.

But in what manner can solid matter, within limits of space which it can but a little transgress, move? We see in a field of wheat, under the wind, or in the waves of a lake : by undulation of contiguous particles. The principles of our undulatory oscillation must, therefore, be continuity and polarity. The movement of the heart is in accordance with these principles.

As a finite being man's activities are a succession of means to *ends* or temporary rests. His thinking activity is, of course, of this kind. By the constitution of it he can arrive at *absolute* rest but in one idea—the idea of *One*. Here is rest because it is the end of all thinking, the result of the smallest division and the largest compound, of all analysis and synthesis. To his thinking function it must therefore be the *summum bonum* and final cause.

Discovering the condition of perfect rest we shall expect that less perfect rests shall be in the ratio of their condition to that condition, and to find the intellect a machine (among other things) for composing multiplicity to unity.

Whatever be the soul, we know it acts by a body that needs alternations of rest. This applies to the whole machine and its parts—to the sensorium as one, and to each sensorial organ. You may tire the sensorium by simultaneous actions without tiring either organ: you may spoil a single organ without spoiling the sensorium.

Both to do and to suffer are kinds of action—*i.e.* transmission. Whatever the nature of force, therefore, it is limited in exercise by the necessity of the body for rest. This necessity is found to be, in the same body, directly as the quantity of force expended.

Change is the measure of force. Much simultaneous change is therefore, as an index, equivalent to less change in longer time. The conditions which oblige absolute rest after a certain expenditure begin to be felt long before that limit. There is an instinctive economy in the sense, that shuns exhaustion and Death. It shrinks from approaching its limit of action—as it shrinks from the longer rest of Death.

There is, therefore, but a small point in time during which sensation is at its best, and the sense is unwilling to undertake any act that diminishes the size of that point: *i.e.* the mind avoids unnecessary *effort*—shuns 'fatigue.'

As this 'point' is diminished by perceiving two instead of one it more willingly perceives one.

Though the Ideal Man constructs the many into the one, there still remains unanswered the *how* and *why* of this construction—the how and why of Proportion, Order, Harmony, Symmetry, Κόσμος.

This is the problem insoluble by reason, and if reason alone could help us the standard of the Ideal would be practically useless.

On what then rely?

On a power in Man of which says Aristotle—('a special power of the immortal Gods') of which says Christianity (Faith?).[1]

What is that power?

Though man in ordinary is chaotic and imperfect, there are men whom a power of temporary transfiguration recomposes towards the Perfect (Man).

Quoad Religious Truths, this new proportion of the functions is Πίστις.

Towards other truths Genius.

[[1] Word omitted in MS.—ED.]

ORIGIN OF RHYTHM, SLEEP, &c

ORIGIN OF RHYTHM.

MAN is distinguished by two cardinal attributes:

1st. That everyone says ' I,' and is conscious of unity in that which so says, however much he may be conscious of multiplicity in his attributes—in qualities necessary to ' I.'

2nd. That his animal life is a systole and diastole—*i.e.* that no healthy man can persevere in action without sleep, or in sleep without action.

To these cardinal conditions all his mechanique conforms, and by them are his notions of externals governed.

From which mechanique come the reasons of Rhythm, of Art, and of Speech.

.

Whether this need (of Sleep) be imposed on the 'soul' by the body, or whether some quality of the principle of life necessitates it in the higher forms of

Incarnation I will not here enquire. I may point out its correspondence with the recurrence of Night and Day, Summer and Winter, and with the undulatory systems of Light, Heat, and Motion.

One result of this principle of alternate action and rest is, that the heart of the higher classes of animals—the most obviously governing organ of the animal body—accomplishes its work by a series of actions and sub-actions, occurring in Man at equal intervals. From this equidistant recurrence of action and sub-action in the dispenser of vivifying blood, it results that the corporeal means by which the 'mind' (or 'soul') acts must,—visibly or not,—accomplish their work in time with the great beater of time: the external and internal organs of sense, for instance, must transact sensation, the mind (or soul) must be affected by the 'outer world,' in a series of actions and sub-actions correlated to those of the heart.

We must keep in mind the great distinction between the organs—as the heart and lungs—in which the collapse answers to true sleep, and those which enjoying what we call 'sleep,' remain so furnished with life-power by the action of heart and lungs as to be able still to act during their quasi-sleep. But these though not 'sleeping' with them, must nevertheless sustain a plus and minus of active ability corresponding with the systole and diastole of the others.

One result of this corporeal ῥύθμος is, that 'external' or internal objects presenting themselves to this equi-beating sensorial action and sub-action should present themselves with their emphatic portions corresponding to the action-beat, or, if in a multiplicity of various values, with their more valuable (emphatic) multiples harmoniously related to the arsis of the beat. Here is the origin of compound rhythm—a motion in which minor motions are contained in a major—and of the simplest relation of parts to a whole.

SLEEP—CHANGE.

Whatever accounts for the need of sleep operates before sleep-point is reached, and all races of men have expressions equivalent to our 'fatigue,' 'weariness,' 'to be tired,' 'to tire,' &c.

All men have also discovered by experiment that the need of sleep comes most quickly upon that kind of doing which we call 'doing exactly the same' and have instinctively lengthened the ability to act by a 'change' of activity.

The originative activity, and its proximate media,

are found to 'tire' most rapidly in actions that are at once sudden and contrary : they seem like a pianist who is relieved by a change of fingering, but who would be exhausted had he to turn from his keyboard to keys behind him.

The law of 'change,' therefore, which dictates relief by 'doing' through media wholly or partially fresh is controlled by other laws. The change must be neither sudden nor contrary, *i.e.* you have the laws of *continuity* and *gradation*.

As the 'originative activity' and its proximate media 'tire' more slowly than the subordinate media, their tendency to change does not arrive till after many changes of those subordinates : *i.e.* you have a principle of perseverance.

The need of Rest is the final cause of ῥυθμός—undulatory rhythm—beats the time of the Beauty music.

The need of change is the final cause of those modifications of undulation which are conditions of higher Beauty.

PERCEPTION AND FEELING.

A Being is that which can be the object of sense (*i.e.* thought or feeling).

The question 'to be' is, therefore, already answered before we can know of its occasion.

For us, therefore, a 'being' is a 'perceptible.'

And the question is not 'existence,' but perceptibility.

Are not all notions of quantity derived from *quantity of feeling*? 'I feel' may stand for any point between these, and would, nevertheless, but for *memory*, be conditioned by no sense of *quantity*. But the sensorium (limited by its mortality, 'rest-need' and 'change-need') furnishes data to experience which react in *vague ideas* of sensational limits, and thence of sensational quantity: *i.e.* of the relation of a given 'I feel' to the whole possible 'I feel.'

PERSONAL IDENTITY.

Every man is, in time present, personally identical with a given person in past time who is, according to the ordinary process of nature, the lineal representative of that person's body and mind—*i.e.* who is, by what is natural to an individual in a given time, the last of an unbroken series of facts of which the first is 'that person.'

THE WILL.

In action there are two parts—that which originates the act and that which performs it.

May not Will be defined as an *attitude* of the *originating* part?

The Will, therefore, is the total attitude of the whole Originator in Man. It is thus distinct from Desire which *may* exist without any motion of the first portion of action.

As trees with leaves should a life show and hide the skeleton principles that shape it.

Of to create in the sense of to be a first cause of substance we have no idea.

Time is the expression of a compound perception of existence and change.

Perhaps the soul is a clear drop of conscious existence capable of various motions.

Perhaps what we call the feelings are a *corpus* to that soul, bearing the relation to it that the body bears to them—acting on it as the body acts on them.

Perhaps this *corpus* dies at Death and the soul, though *potentially* all that it was before, ceases to be actively, because having nothing to put it in relation with exciting causes.

Perhaps resurrection from the Dead is a reconstruction of this *corpus*.

Perhaps the soul is as a dewdrop, having no light or colour in itself but receiving the Light of God which it reflects and refracts. That Light, contained and reflected by it, is at once not its own absolutely and its own relatively, and though not caused by it is influenced in manifestation by the state and size of the dewdrop.

NOTES ON THE RELATION OF LANGUAGE AND THOUGHT.

[THE greater bulk of the Philological Memoranda left by Mr. Dobell are too merely memoranda for the writer's own use, data for his further study and observation, to be available for printing. The few that have been selected are brought together from various notebooks.—ED.]

I seem to see a homology between some of the deeper morphological truths—animal and vegetable—and the mutations and essential laws of language.

Suppose Creation to be, as it were, an involuntary Act, bearing, like language, impress of the idiosyncrasy of What secerned it?

———

That is true Speech, heard or seen, which produces in the percipient the attitude of mind produced by the thing spoken of.

Is not this the secret of spoken language?

In such language the resemblance of 'sound to sense'

is not primarily in the *sound* but in the organic action by which the sound is produced and which produces in him who *acts* a certain attitude of mind. And he who *hears* undergoes the same attitude by virtue of his knowledge—(unconscious—and by experience)—of the action by which the sound he hears would be produced if he had uttered it.

In the formation and transmutation of words we have to consider two systems of causes.

I. Physical, calculable from physical conditions in the organs of Language—cerebral and oral : from this are deducible general laws of origin and change.

II. Metaphysical,—the motive forces of the human soul : from these are deducible the specific disturbances of general laws.

PHYSICS OF SPEECH.

By external visible bodily gesture men can express themselves. Why? Because certain movements of the body are accompanied by movements of the mind, and the 'hearer'—*i.e.* the observer—knowing what these are in himself understands what they express from another.

But there is an invisible, yet physical, gesticulation,

having an intimate co-action of the soul, and capable of subtleties so fine that the eye, at a little distance, could hardly detect and with certainty discriminate them. This is the gesticulation of the organs of the throat and mouth. It is *indicated* by sounds produced by it, but the value of those sounds is not as sounds, but as indices of organic motions which answer to mental movements.

As these organs are part of the body the principles of the physics of speech must be, primarily, those common to the whole body in its interaction with the soul. Secondarily those deducible from the nature of the organs themselves. Thirdly any disturbances of these resulting from any of the properties of sound.

SPEECH VERBAL.

Man puts the ideas of things into words like themselves—*i.e.* like things. But how can words be like things. By imitative sound?

No. This could apply but to few things, and even in regard to them would be a mean imitation—not art.

Things have either size, shape, weight, colour, &c., rapidity, &c. These attributes are associated in our minds not only with their visual images (where visual) but with certain feelings—*e.g.* weight with difficulty, size with comprehension, shape with pleasure, when easy of perception, (*et per contra*), colour with more complex emotions.

It is in so far as the positions and action of the *organs of speech* produce in us the sensations which suggest the attributes of the things signified by words that words resemble things.

This they do both by imitating those attributes, where imitable, and by so moving or posing themselves as to produce in us the associated feelings.

Sense is represented by sound in various ways.

I. Imitation, the lowest of all because substituting an untruth (as an end) for the Truth, instead of suggesting the actual Truth by some non-truth as a means.

II. By producing the same state of mind as the thing represented would produce—and this is done in various ways—by sounds that have essential connection with certain attitudes of mind, or by sounds that, by *suggesting certain acts of the organs of utterance*, influence the feelings, or by *rhythm* that, through various laws, affects the whole human system.

After a language has been formed on the principles of dumb-show it becomes an object of tuition (oral or graphic) and thus of those physical principles which modify bodily action and interaction (inertia, &c., &c.), and those mental principles which modify the ideas which are expressed by bodily action.

We must not, therefore, always expect to find the word that answers to an idea in a cultivated language (or one received by conquest *et hoc genere*) the best dumb-show representative of that idea; but on investigation we shall find that it represents some word that *has* been such dumb-show representative.

PERMUTATION OF IDEAS.

In the Sacred Language of the far east *Ahm-an*—, an audible sigh, is the word for the soul.

Hear the same sigh in ἄνεμος—the Ahm no wider or longer than α : ν the mouth subsiding towards rest— ε the smaller spiration of the remaining breath through the narrow aperture—μ the close of the lips.

Ahm becomes, therefore, ανεμ (ος being added for case-ending). I perceive the law of permutation is in the direction from action towards inaction: but action is change, change is a measure of force. The law, therefore, is in the direction from more force to less—from strength to weakness.

What the strong do from indolence we may study in what the weak do from incapacity.

By physiological causes it is probable that the descendants of a nation that said *aham* for I, would continue to gesticulate similarly for similar expressions, because of inheriting a similar brain, and a gesticulating machine apt, by special development, to such gesticulation.

That, to speak popularly, the true object of the speaking mind in putting in motion the speaking machine is not the production of audible sounds but the satisfaction of certain dispositions to gesticulate with the organs of speech which follow certain agitations of the human consciousness, produced by the same originative action, cerebral, nervine and muscular, as commences all bodily violence.

May not the causes which limit transmutation of Species be analogous to those which determine the intermutations of language? A given word undergoes modifications limited by the mutability of its letters, and that mutability depends on the shape and character of the organs which produce the Sounds they represent.

Memorandum.—To apply that principle, regarding

compounds, &c., which proves Sanscrit to be the oldest of known Languages, to systems of ideas. In doing so remember Chavier's description of the effect upon speech of the change from the Sanscrit to the Chaldaic mode of writing—and remember that the Etruscan plan of writing was from left to right.

FIRST PERSONAL PRONOUN.

' I ' is the unknown antecedent of consciousness, and being entirely unknown is, like a mathematical point, destitute of all parts and of all qualities except such as we infer of it from its effects. The reactionary result of these is, therefore, a quasi-notion of ' I ' as a simple unit.

Its name in most languages expresses the *beginner*, usually the beginner of motion—'ἐγώ' 'EGO'—*i.e.* that which says g-hard—the strongest expulsory movement of the speech-machinery—' ich '—(the next strongest)—' je ' formerly, doubtless, j, being pronounced as Spanish j. The Italian Io, is not an original creation, being mollified ego—' I ' is the same.

Taking as postulate that man is a sentient being I do not define ' to feel.'

Of ' I ' as merely existence, I at rest, we can know

nothing. Our knowledge commences at 'I feel' and 'I do.'

MYTHS.

That part of a Myth which contains a human faculty is its root-stem.

After tracing the root-stems of all Myths to the universal human faculties there will, in any non-indigenous, remain terminations, suffixes and affixes, not accountable by the constitution of the people or the nature of the indigenous external world.

———

(The province of Poetry.) All Language is an expression of relation : every generic noun, every adjective, which recognizes a quality already known. But as language is for ordinary minds it expresses *obvious* relations. You require a language for extraordinary perceptions and that language is Poetry.

———

The truest analogue to those unteleogic facts in the Natural World which modern science is continually discovering is to be found in the facts of human language as brought into light by such men as Grimm, Bopp, &c.

Is then the universe a Divine Language amenable to

conditions similar in nature though differing in time and space?

If so, do the Functions of God answer to the races of Men, the inferior borrowing, as it were, a grammar from the higher and using it under the modifications of other spheres of action?

RELIGIOUS

RELIGIOUS.[1]

Whatsoever things are true for Man the Immortal I call Religion, and, in this sense, Religion is the only worthy object of human Study.

THEORETIC.

SUPPOSING there were no such thing as *words* what idea should we have of an Invisible God?

We should have ideas of His *effects* and of such of the Attributes producing such effects as we could feel in ourselves by our possession of the same.

But of the Total Agent what?

I think only a dim Image, the reflection of *our consciousness of our own existence*: or the result of the effort of the mind to conceive, which effort may produce the

---

[1] It has been judged fitting to publish, in such a volume as the present, only a small proportion of the comments on texts, &c., contained in Mr. Dobell's notebooks. It may be interesting to some readers to know that Mr. Dobell's study of the Bible, especially in early life, had been so close and constant as to have made his memory master of the whole of the New Testament.—ED.

vague figure of its own action; a shape on the corrugating brain; an impression on the soul, like that of the wind on water. Therefore in reality none.

A spiritual world, then, could only be directly apprehended in so far as it agreed with our own faculties and experience.

Dismissing, therefore, as mere shadows and reflections of ourselves, all intellectual notions of the spiritual world, what, apart from words, remains as testimony to it?

This: that from the top and culmen of all perception the mind as it were stretches up arms into vacancy, desires *towards*—what?

The testimony therefore to the unknown is of *feeling*.

Does not each Divine Dispensation contain in addition to its own economy a Member of the economy that is to succeed it?

I am not speaking of prefigurements, but of some fact only to be explained by the context of the succeeding system and, therefore, rightly viewed, a guarantee of that successor. A member by which the one is to be morticed to the other. They, therefore, who attempt (as the Trinitarians) to theorize these facts, and bend what was intended as a *projection* into the framework of the economy cannot succeed; and, in the attempt, do violence to the Divine Scheme of Progression. The Unitarians, on the other hand, are apt to ignore the historical connection.

THE FIRST ADVENT.

For any fact of History to be seen and understood truly, it must be contemplated from at least two points of view.

One, the human, which has its *locus standi* before the catastrophe, in the *fons* and *origo* of the action; and the other, that of the Philosophy of History, which has its *locus* long afterwards.

In the case of remote facts the first of these points of view is often altogether lost, and our idea of the fact becomes necessarily hemispheric.

This has doubtless happened with the great fact of the first Advent. We see it solely from the optimist and philosophical stand-point and have almost lost what was to its contemporaries its chief practical character—an appeal to the suffrages of the Jewish people. An appeal which, like all such appeals, must be made, and—whatever His prescience—was made, *on the hypothesis of success*.

The refusal of those suffrages (in any National completeness) is (in its effect upon the Action) one of the most important facts of the Gospel-History.

Christ did not, humanly speaking, *come* to be rejected, crucified, raised. 'If thou couldst have known in this thy day *the things pertaining to thy peace.*'

If the princes of this world had known the true mystery of the Gospel 'they *would not* have crucified the Lord of Glory.'

We should expect therefore to find this system constructed on the hypothesis of a present Lord. A Gospel of Life and Work, not of Death and disappointment.

In the case of a blight we do not take the blighted product to be the law of the fruit.

FALSITY OF ARGUMENT FROM SUCCESS.

The acknowledgment that Christianity is Divine because it has proved Itself the mode by which God governs is really valueless, because it is an argument from Success (which could be used in other cases *ad absurdum*) and because, like all arguments from success, it furnishes no claim on Human acceptance before the era of success.

We require a proof that would be equally a proof in the first year of Evangelism.

ABSOLUTENESS OF BELIEF, IN THE APOSTLES, TESTIFIED TO BY MANNER OF THEIR ARGUMENT.

One of the intrinsic testimonies to the truth of what the Apostles believed is the non-demonstrative and improbative manner in which they argued for it.

By being nearly always rhetoricians, and using evidence not for what it is worth but for what it will fetch, they demonstrate beyond all other means of proof the confidence of their own belief.

They speak as men so absolutely certain, in virtue of other evidence, that the kind of proof adducible by writing is merely valuable in so far as it uses predispositions of the hearers and persuades them, being blind, to yield to the men who see.

DEVELOPABLE NATURE OF CHRISTIANITY.

If it had been intended at the introduction of Christianity to institute a permanent undevelopable outward system for it, would not the first care of the Apostles have been to engrave the formula on tables of stone?

That the formula, if made, has *not come down to us* is no argument against the above intention, but the evidence we have that *no such formula was made* or thought of seems a strong argument. It is not merely that the

Apostles seem to have taken insufficient means to eave such a formula but the case is more than negative :—the means taken to send down their doctrine—and manifestly taken under the impression that they were sufficient—are inconsistent with the possibility of such formula.

THE CATHOLIC THEORY OF A SUCCESSIONAL CHURCH.

If Christ intended 'the Church' to be His embodied word He must have intended its principles and practice to change or not. If not to change then the Catholic Church is invalid. If to change then to change according to mere natural process or by special Divine guidance. If the first [by mere natural process?] then all the various heresies and perversions authentic. If the second [by special Divine guidance?] reformation is impossible.

PROTESTANT THEORY OF A SCRIPTURAL CREED.

Does God design such a creed?

God is always consistent with Himself.

Design is evidenced by adaptation of means to ends and, in the natural world therefore, is shown by the selection of 'means' which, according to His own Natural ordinances, will be followed by those ends.

It may be said, God designs the special sanction of

this miracle of preservation. But it may be answered that this would apply to Catullus, the Pandects, Plautus, the preserved books of Livy, &c., &c.

It may be said God designs each soul to find its own creed out of the Record. If so we are safe in deposing to what we find *and no more*.

Does not a collation of every creed bring one to that conclusion which, according to my theory, is the true result of a true study of the written Gospel, and show therefore the congruity of the written and the embodied Word?

VALUE OF FREEDOM OF THOUGHT IN SCRIPTURE READING.

Does not the value of Scripture reading to the ordinary mind depend on the *absence* of any search for Doctrinal discovery?

On mental repose as to the credenda?

This repose is only possible on such a neutral creed as above suggested.

Textual support of theory (negative creed et cetera) [1] to be found—

---

[1] One of the fundamental distinctions of this 'negative or neutral Creed' would have been the absence of any attempt to dogmatize, or even to theorize, as to the 'exact nature' of Christ.—ED.

Luke x. 22. 'No man knoweth who the Son is, but the Father.'

John x. 29 et seq. : 'My Father, which gave them me, is greater than all : and no man is able to pluck them out of my Father's hand. I and my Father are one.'

John xi. 15. '*I* was not *there*.'

John xii. 45. 'And he that seeth me, seeth him that sent me.'

John xiv. from 7 to 11. 'If ye had known me, ye should have known my Father also : and from henceforth ye know him, and have seen him.'

CATHOLICISM AND PROTESTANTISM.

Catholicism is (potentially) great, beautiful, wise powerful, one of the most consistent and congruous constructions man has made ; but it is not educational and will, therefore, die ; nay, must be killed as pernicious in proportion to its excellence.

Protestantism is narrow, ugly, impudent, unreasonable, inconsistent, incompatible : a babel of logomachy and literalism : a wrangling club of half-thinking pedants, half-taught geniuses, and untaught egotists of every type : the nursery of conceit and fanaticism : the holiday ground of all the 'fools that rush in.'

But it is educational and therefore it will live ; nay, must be fed and housed, cared for and fought for, as the *sine quâ non* of the spiritual life of Man.

LOGOS.

The Chaldee paraphrasts use Memra in many of those places where Moses says God : *e.g.* those wherein God is said to have created, appeared, or spoken. In all such cases God was *expressed*; and Memra (the word) was well put for that phenomenon which was His expression.

In the total universe He is also expressed, doubtless; but only organically in any one of its *parts* : but in these miraculous appearances HE, as distinct from any one or more of His Attributes, is represented, as in a focus or miniature.

The pagans saw the same truth when they spoke of Cosmos and Microcosmos.

It is a noble testimony to the profoundness with which the Paraphrasts believed in an Invisible God that they found themselves compelled to use another name when He was spoken of as perceptible to the senses.

Whoever endeavours to follow out the subtle relationship of a Divine *Phenomenon* and its imperceptible

Substans will understand why the sayings of Christ of Himself can never be apprehended, and could not, nevertheless, have been other than they are.

There may be a unity of the Memra, Logos, or Expression, but a variety and individuality in the several acts of it. As my voice to-day and yesterday is the same, but the utterances are distinct. Ὁ λόγος θεοῦ created the Worlds, ὁ λόγος θεοῦ was crucified on Calvary, but it by no means follows that Christ is that utterance of the λόγος at which the worlds came into being.

'Ambassadors are the Word of the Prince who sends them.'—*Montesquieu.*

May not John 1 be thus explained.

Ὁ λόγος is the Divine function of Language. That Attribute or Quality whereby the Divine Nature is utterable. In the universe It expressed Itself: but in those later days It had used the perfect language of an 'Express Image,'—the visible and audible Son of God.

As Plato had used Ὁ λόγος there may be an allusion to his doctrine and an indication of the portion of Truth contained in it.

COMMENTS ON CORINTHIANS I.

In 1 Corinthians i.—The distinction between the two methods by which Truth can be received is made strong. Revelation and Deduction.

Verse 2.—'With all that in every place call upon the name of Jesus Christ.' Note the comprehensiveness of the tolerated variety.

Verse 10.—' I beseech you—that ye all speak the same thing.' Note, at the same time, the unity of the ideal standard.

Verses 20 (' Hath not God made foolish the wisdom of this world?') 21, 26, 27, and 28, 'and base things of the world, and things which are despised, hath God chosen, yea, and things which are not, to bring to nought things that are :'

It requires to bear in mind the 'World' of which this is spoken. Of a different world (in the sense of non-church) it might not be true.

Verse 23. 'But we preach Christ crucified, unto the Jews a stumbling block, and unto the Greeks foolishness.'

The Philosophies of Heathendom had not perceived that not a *Theorem* but a *Man* was the moral desideratum of Mankind : *i.e.* (verse 24)—'Christ the power of God and the wisdom of God.' The *embodied* Wisdom of God: in whom (verse 30. ' But of him are ye in Christ Jesus, who of God is made unto us wisdom ')—Man and God *at one.*

Chap. ii. 8. 'For had they known it they would *not have crucified the Lord of Glory.*' What becomes then of the suffering and expiation of Christ as the *sine quâ non* of the Providential Scheme?

ILLUSTRATIONS OF GENERAL PRINCIPLES CONTAINED IN SPECIAL APPLICATIONS.

Compare Luke xii. 22 to 40 ('Therefore I say unto you, take no thought for your life, what ye shall eat: neither for the body, what ye shall put on),' with the texts concerning diligence in business and providing for your own household, and St. Paul's exhortation as to 'working with our hands.'

Compare Luke xiv. 12 ('When thou makest a dinner or a supper call not thy friends, nor thy brethren),' with the many exhortations to hospitality and community *quoad friends and brethren* elsewhere.

Compare Luke xiv. 20 (in which ' I have married a wife and therefore I cannot come,' is given as one of the condemned excuses) with Christ's dictum concerning matrimony and Paul's description of conjugal love.

THEORETIC. 159

In stating one principle out of many the statement should be absolute and ideal. The limitations will come by the modifying action of other co-equal principles. 'If any man will take thy coat let him take thy cloak also,' so far as *freedom in giving* and absence of malice are concerned. But not interdicting that controlling power of other principles which would never allow the full action of this.

As scientific illustration of application of principles take *undulatory* rectitude, in light, sound, &c. As familiar illustration of the mode in which general principles are specifically applicable, take Dress. Each rank and occupation should dress in different forms, but the Principles of cleanliness, grace, harmony, congruity, are common to all those special applications, and are more obeyed in the variety of application than in a uniformity.

ARE GENERAL PRINCIPLES INTENDED FOR UNIVERSAL APPLICATION?

'God willeth not the death of a sinner but rather that he should turn to Him and live?' Therefore the Principles must be such as if universally applied would be for the universal benefit of society.

But perhaps, in the event of such application, a

miraculous interposition would adapt the material world to the new wants of mankind?

Would God frame a material Cosmos on such elaborate and well-established 'Laws,' and frame a moral Cosmos that should need the abrogation of those Laws?

THEOCRACY.

As it is when the common flesh and blood has subtilized into brain that the Spirit can alone dwell therein, may it not be that the fine perfection of human institutions will be the event and *sine quâ non* at which Theocracy shall commence?

THE KINGDOM OF GOD.

To understand the double sense in which the title is used in Scripture must we not remember that every human *congeries* before it can become objective must first exist subjectively? Conversion which is internal must precede, singularly and without 'observation,' the external appearance and action of a *body* of *converts*, and this applies especially to such an *Imperium in Imperio* as the Kingdom of God. Keeping this in mind read and compare the following—

Luke xix. 11—'And as they heard these things, he added and spake a parable, because he was nigh to

Jerusalem, and *because they thought that the Kingdom of God should immediately appear.'*

Luke xxii. 16. ·'For I say unto you I will not any more eat thereof until it be fulfilled in the Kingdom of God,' *et seq.* :

Luke ix. 2. 'And he sent them to preach the Kingdom of God, and to heal the sick.' (And observe how minute the instructions, as to material things, which follow. We may conclude thence that if anything spiritually important had been included in them it would have been recorded, and may infer, therefore, that the Gospel they were to preach was not a Gospel of doctrine, but, like the Evangel of the seventy—'the Kingdom of God is at hand.')

Luke x. 11—'Even the very dust of your city, which cleaveth on us, we do wipe off against you : notwithstanding be ye sure of this, that the Kingdom of God is come nigh unto you.'

xiii. 21. 'It (the Kingdom of God) is like leaven, which a woman took and hid in three measures of meal, till the whole was leavened.'

'For I tell you of a truth there be *some* standing here which shall not taste of Death *till* they see the Kingdom of God.' Luke ix. 27.

It is evident therefore that the 'Kingdom' which

the Apostles proclaimed was a future Kingdom, and that when we are told the 'Kingdom of God is within us,' the whole Kingdom is not meant, or the word is used in another sense.

See also Luke xi. 20: 'if I with the finger of God cast out devils, no doubt the Kingdom of God *hath come upon you.*'

'HARD SAYINGS' OF CHRIST.

As an example of the 'hard sayings' spoken by Christ, with intention to perplex and thus winnow his hearers, take John vi. 35, to 58—(beginning 'I am the bread of life, he that cometh to me shall never hunger; and he that believeth on me shall never thirst,' ending 'he that eateth of this bread shall live for ever')—and find the principle of solution in v. 63—'It is the spirit that quickeneth: the flesh profiteth nothing: the words that I speak unto you they are spirit, and they are life.'

NOTÆ. INSPIRATION, &C.

The state of mind in Men indubitably '*inspired*' should be carefully studied in St. Peter's own account of the mental process by which he arrived at his duty towards the friends of Cornelius. It is singularly different from what would be popularly expected.

To speak of being saved through the blood of Christ is to use that common figure by which the part is put for the whole. We are saved through that Life which would not have been perfect but for the Death; the Death therefore is that essential *part* which in using such a figure must be employed.

Observe the remarkable truth evidently to be inferred from Luke xix. 42. 'If thou hadst known, even thou, at least in this thy day, the things which belong unto thy peace' and 1 Corinthians ii. 8, 'which none of the princes of this world knew: for had they known it, they would not have crucified the Lord of glory'—that if Israel had received Him, and He had not been crucified, His mission would have been no less fulfilled.

The statement that to him who hath shall be given is explicable by *Luke's* version of the Parable. All the servants started with *one* talent—the ultimate difference was due to individual merit—'They say unto him Lord he *hath* ten talents.' The answer is 'to him' *i.e.* of those servants—'that hath' *i.e. so* hath, by meritorious exertion—'shall be given.'

Luke xxii. 35. 'When I sent you without purse, and scrip, and shoes, lacked ye anything?' Is not this the point of departure for the new Life of the Apostles, when no longer associated with their Lord? Does He not here indicate that, whereas their previous state with Him had been superhuman and exceptional, henceforth they were remitted to the common life of man? Hitherto they had, doubtless, eaten of the miraculous Loaves and Fishes; but henceforth they were to consider the power of miracle as sacred to impersonal and non-selfish uses.

Was not this new line of demarcation necessary in leaving them to themselves? And did they ever afterwards transgress it?

This view of the significance of these verses seems confirmed by the injunction respecting the swords being sufficiently fulfilled ('it is enough') by the 'two swords'—*i.e.* by two of the company being armed.

The injunction had no relation to aggressive or exceptional action, but merely to that state of defence which was necessary to the safe conduct of life—*e.g.* to secure travelling in a country of banditti, &c., &c.

The preamble to Christ's command *quoad* the Swords 'when I sent,' &c. is invaluable as showing the *limit* to a previous command that had, *in se*, all the appearance of universality.

Christ's mode of reasoning with the Jews is a demonstration founded on their own axioms and postulates; using them logically *without thereby authorizing them as truths*. And we shall see that this mode was unavoidable, for had He to establish His own Premisses He would never (in the allotted time and space) have reached any conclusions at all. And this mode would appear the more eligible to one who could perceive the absolute Truth of things and know, therefore, the necessary fallacy of the truest human statement—*e.g.* answers about John the Baptist: healing on Sabbaths: David and the Shew Bread: Beelzebub.

The fact that he whom the Apostles took for Christ (after the Crucifixion) *did* and *obtained* nothing which would recompense an impostor for the pains and hazard of simulating Him is weighty evidence that their belief was just. Viewed thus the poverty of the post-mortem portion of the History—so far as acts and teachings are concerned—is among the most powerful proofs of its truth.

Christianity does not ignore or disclaim the 'natural' virtues: on the contrary they are the egg and bud out of which the others are to develop and effloresce. The new birth is a *Transfiguration*.

As the *mens sana* to the *corpus sanum*, so should the

Christian grace be to the 'natural' virtue it warms and lights.

They therefore who take on a grace specifically Christian without that natural quality which is its natural antecedent, which is, in fact, itself in a lower stage, are guilty of ὑπόκρισις.

He who is just, generous, brave, may rise to Christian honour, to the love and charity of Christianity, and to its most exalted heroisms. But the appearance of these climacteric graces without the co-existence of the others is morbid and unreal.

Christ illustrates the necessity of the moral *corpus sanum* as an antecedent when He chose the hearty fishermen of Galilee, and left the Pharisees of Jerusalem.

Marcellus built a temple to Virtus approached through a Temple to Honour.

The spontaneities (as well as duties) of the Christian should act in a continual consciousness of the *character* of God. This action under patronage—to adapt the vulgar phrase—saves the spontaneities from egotism.

(*Baptism.*) Observe in Acts vi. that the possession of the Holy Spirit *preceded* the *imposition of the Apostle's hands*. Observe, also, that the possession of it in the case of the friends of Cornelius, and in the preceding cases, was so externally evident as to be unmistakable. Also that the Descent of the Spirit preceded baptism. Baptism therefore can have no essential necessity.

Christianity had to supersede two great Pagan systems—the morality of the Philosophers—teleologic and material—and the sensuous worship of the popular Religion. It was opposed to both, but more essentially to the former. It had nearer relation to the immorality of natural aberration than to the artificial distortions and essential selfishness of Phariseeism.

It is important to perceive that some facts to-day stand for different things from those signified in Apostolic times—*e.g.* v. Luke xiv.—we give a feast now not as a virtuous action in the sense of charity but as an *expression* of certain things. Such a feast comes under entirely new principles.

So of Dress which having become a language is amenable to those principles which govern all virtuous expression.

The Jews had exalted the *machinery* of spiritual education from a means to an end; they therefore counted the reward of every action. We look for 'reward' from the end, not the means, from what we *are* not what we do.

This difference explains many difficulties in Christ's teaching,—which had to deal with the Jewish mistake.

NOTES ON ROMANS.

Chaps. i. and ii. The Apostle sets forth that, though misbelief is generally followed by misconduct, goodness, the proper consequence of orthodoxy, may exist without its usual antecedent; see also Chap. iii. 29, 'Is He the God of the Jews only? is He not also of the Gentiles?' Wherefore since the end and not the means is the *sine quâ non* there is no *necessary* inequality between Jew and Gentile. And since, whether with the means or without the means, the end has generally been missed, it is evident that all existing means have been insufficient and that both provinces of Mankind are in need of something new.

That 'something new' is the substitution of Principle for Law, and the acceptance of a faithful Ego, devoted to God, instead of that harmonious federation of human faculties, bodily and mental, which, as an obedient total, was the only human Being previously acceptable—*i.e.* justification by Faith instead of by Works.

In Chap. iv. The Apostle proceeds to show that this acceptance was anterior to the Law, and of a wider and higher originality, since Abraham himself was by it first united to God. That the Law therefore was a decadence from a higher, nobler and older mode of intimacy between God and Man : and therefore that Faith is not, as the Jews would be likely to claim, an exclusive result and privilege of Judaism.

In Chap. v. The Apostle points out the joyful and thankful attitude of a soul united to God by Faith.

In Chap. vi. He provides against the antinomian dangers of the Doctrine of Faith—showing 'after the manner of men' (verse 19) by the allegory of Death and Servitude the obligations of the Justified.

In Chap. vii. verse 15 to the end—the Apostle seems to set forth the great truth of the federal nature of the Human Mind. The Ego is recognised as distinct (see especially verse 15, 'For that which I do I allow not ; for what I would, that I do not ; but what I hate that I do ;' and 22 'For I delight in the law of God after the *inward man* ;') from many of its faculties, as a head is distinct from its members.

The recognition of this *imperium in imperio*, this sanctuary within unclean outer courts, this just man in Sodom, this inner saint in the outward sinner must have changed the whole theory of Divine Government. If there be Human Beings in whom it does not exist this difference would afford a criterion by which Humanity could be divided in two classes : those in whom the Divine element having a ποῦ στῶ—could eventually leaven the evil, and those who, humanly speaking, are hopeless.

In Chap. viii. The same idea continued.

In these chapters the theory by which the sinner can grow into the saint is for the first time opened to mankind.

All other moralities, viewing him as a unity, hand him over to the vengeance of the violated Law. Here, by recognizing a 'spirit which is life because of righteousness' even when the rebellious body is 'dead because of sin,' we have the first condition of growth—*i.e.* a nucleus that may, with time, assimilate the incongruous elements.

For the first time Hope is held out to the unsuccessful aspirant for Goodness, and a life outwardly sinful is brought within the pale of Virtue.

From verse 28 'and we know that all things work together for good to them that love God'—to the end, a pæan of that gratitude natural to a soul so delivered.

In Chap. ix. A further demonstration of what was shown in Chap. iv.—that even in the chosen seed the secret of Divine choice was *meta*-physical : that God has always vindicated a Prerogative above the Law of Human Works. And a justification of God therein. Also an implied admission that *election—e.g.* verse 23—('and that He might make known the riches of His glory on the vessels of mercy, which He had before prepared unto glory,') involves *preparation* : *i.e.* is not arbitrary.

A great deal of the quaint and struggling expression of these two chapters resolves itself into the endeavour to enunciate for the first time an unrecognised distinction— *i.e.* that between a Life according to *Principles* (*e.g.* Chap. viii. verses 6 'For to be carnally minded is death ; but to be spiritually minded is life and peace,' and 11 'But if the Spirit of Him that raised up Jesus from the dead dwell in you, He that raised up Christ from the dead shall also quicken your mortal bodies by His Spirit that dwelleth in you,') and a Life according to Law.

Verses 29, beginning 'For whom He did foreknow,' 30, 33, of Chap. viii. and 9-19 of Chap. ix. are easily explicable when once we divest criminality of those attributes which are the mere reflexes of our exclusively Human instincts, look on it with those faculties only which we have in common with God, and recognize the purely emendatory nature of ' Punishment.'

When ' Punishment' is seen as merely a creative process it falls into the category of all the other second-causes of development: and 'election' and 'predestination' explain themselves.

In Chaps. x. and xi. the Apostle works to show that the suppression of Israel is temporary, and indeed—xi. 16-25—more apparent than real, inasmuch as though a generation is cast away the unchangeable root remains in the earth and supports the Modern Church.

Nota bene Chap. x. 9, the Golden Formula of Faith. 'If thou shalt confess with thy mouth the Lord Jesus, and shalt believe in thine heart that God hath raised Him from the dead, thou shalt be saved.'

The argument in Chap. vii. 17, ('Now then it is no more I that do it, but sin that dwelleth in me,') is that of Shakespeare in Hamlet Act V. Scene II. 'was't Hamlet wronged Laertes?'

Running through the whole Letter is, as it were, an underplot of argument to show that though the creed of Israel has lapsed Israel Itself is undegraded.

Chap. xii. Having previously set forth the 'Mercies of God' the Apostle claims the ethical results of gratitude. And what Religion or Philosophy can show such a chapter of Morals on considerations so pure?

Chap. xiii. verses 1, 2, 3, 4, 6, beginning 'Let every soul be subject unto the higher powers,' probably are specific and refer to the Roman ruler of the day. If not, *nota bene* the '*powers* that *be*' are 'ordained'—not the simulacra thereof. And, in any wise, bring me the '*power*' that answers the definition in verse 3, 4, and 6, and I will admit all the rest concerning him.

[The following passage on the same subject occurs among the historical notes for the Drama. -ED.]

(*False Claims.*) 'The powers that be.'

The quotation of Boniface VIII., in the Bull Unam Sanctam, of Romans xiii. 'The powers that be are ordained of God,' in the sense of *ordinated*, is proved to be a mis-construction by the verse, and succeeding verses, in which τάσσω is used in various forms and *combinations* all indicating its primitive sense to be to place or *set* (without *relation*).

Memorandum on that verse. It had relation to a pagan Emperor with whom Christians could have no political relation *pro* or *con*. These Emperors were not hereditary. It might have been written in Nero's five first (good) years. Whatever its meaning the Prince *who fulfils St. Paul's description* ('not a terror to good works, but to the evil. Wilt thou then not be afraid of the power? do that which is good, and thou shalt have praise of the same. For he is the minister of God to thee for good. But if thou do that which is evil, be afraid; for he beareth not the sword in vain : for he is the minister of God, a revenger to execute wrath upon him that doeth evil.' 'For they are God's ministers, attending continually upon this very thing,') will be worthy of allegiance : and to no other can it apply.

Chap. xiii. 8 to 10, beginning 'owe no man anything, but to love one another,' ending 'therefore love is the fulfilling of the law.' This simple exhortation of a universal *principle* is a worthy *sequitur* to the intellectual exposition of government by Principles wherewith the first part of the Epistle is occupied.

Chap. xiv. This invaluable chapter sets forth that sliding scale of *practice* which is the inevitable result of a Life from Principle.

Chap. xv. Beginning 'We then that are strong ought to bear the infirmities of the weak, and not to please ourselves.' Inestimably expounds that sympathy by which alone the embryologic Law is consistent with social action.

'SACRIFICE.'

Is there a case in the Old Testament wherein the thing sacrificed did not *belong* to the person who was to benefit by the offering?

The emendatory theory of Punishment is inconsistent with a Vicar.

The idea of substitution is founded (in Greeks and others) on the belief that the effect of sacrifice is upon God instead of upon Man.

If the offering were a debt to God, valuable to Him *per se*, of course it could be paid by substitution.

In rising up the scale of human perfection we come to the perfect character, but, magnify the qualities of this as we will, the human intellect can still conceive of them only as within limits, *e.g.*, as Immense Goodness, Immense Power.

To reach not the Idea but the nearest that we have to an Idea of God, we have, as it were, to remove the bounds of these Qualities, and try in vain to think of unbounded Power—unbounded Goodness. We can, as it were, destroy the bound, but we cannot follow the disbounded Attribute in its expansion.

The first is Christ, the Second God.

Christ, therefore, is God made flesh—*i.e.* God within the bounds of human idea—the bounds which, like a mould, the human mind imposes on Infinite Substance.

MEMORANDA CONCERNING THE TRINITY.

First. That if the *pre-existence* of Christ could be proved, it would have nothing to do with His *Godhead*.

Second. All sects agree that the Jews did not believe in a Trinity.

Therefore if Christ intended to introduce so great, so vital, so wonderful a change of belief, He would have made it the most striking and often repeated doctrine of His teaching. He would have given us the plainest and most frequent declarations, not left it to be inferred from a few scattered and ambiguous passages.

Thirdly. He has Himself been at pains to explain most lucidly *the way* in which He was one with His Father. See John xvii. 11, 22, 23, 'that they may be one *even as* (in the manner in which) We are one.'

A spiritual oneness. A oneness in object and love.

Fourth. Our English Version was made by men who *already believed in the Trinity*. All the passages which (as in all Classic Languages) were susceptible of two interpretations were of course, therefore, translated according to that reading which best agreed with their preconceived Ideas.

Fifth. The translation (therefore) of those passages which are quoted in favour of *the Unity* cannot be, and never has been, disputed, because they were translated by the *Trinitarians themselves*.

Sixth. But there are more than *fifty* (fifty-eight I think) other passages which if translated and read properly would be in favour of the Unity.

And these fifty include every passage quoted by the Trinitarians in favour of the Trinity.

FRAGMENTARY MEMORANDA CONCERNING BAPTISM.

Baptism has nothing to do with water.

If *literal* Baptism had been an *ordinance* we should have had all detail.

If it mattered whether water or spirit, then it also mattered *how* administered.

'I indeed baptize you with water unto repentance,' 'He shall baptize you with the Holy Ghost, and with fire.' Matthew iii. 11.

'The same is he that baptizeth with the Holy Ghost.' John i. 33.

We must, therefore, look for a *spiritual* sense.

'The like figure whereunto baptism doth also now save

us, not the putting away of the filth of the flesh, but the answer of a good conscience toward God.' 1 Peter iii. 21.

'John baptized with the baptism of repentance.' Acts xix. 4.

'According to his mercy he saved us by the washing of regeneration, and renewing of the Holy Ghost.' Titus iii. 5.

'Ye have put off the old man with his deeds.' Colossians iii. 9.

[Baptism, therefore, repentance, regeneration, putting off of old man, shown to be synonymous terms.]

Now *what* can this *belief* do? 'Then said he to the multitude that came forth to be baptized, bring forth therefore fruits worthy of repentance, and begin not to say within yourselves, we have Abraham for our father: for I say unto you, that God is able of these stones to raise up children unto Abraham.'

'The axe is laid unto the root of the trees:' a selection even from the select.

John's knowledge of his mission—

'I indeed baptize you with water,' 'he shall baptize you with the Holy Ghost and with fire.'

[Quotations giving various uses of the word 'baptized.']

'The mind is enlarged by labours suited to its strength, but is *baptized* by such as exceed its power.'—*Plutarch.*

'On account of the abundant supply from these sources, they do not *baptize* the people with taxes.'—*Diodorus.*

'I am one of those who have been baptized by that great wave of Calamity.'—*Liban.*

'And baptized with the Calamity.'—*Heliodorus.*

'Iniquity baptizes (overwhelms) me.'—*Isaiah.*

'He who bears with difficulty the burden he already has, would be entirely baptized by a small addition.'—*Liban.*

FRAGMENT OF A 'CREED.'

That in a certain age of the World appeared a Personage.

'No man knoweth who the Son is——.'

That He was surrounded by attestation from the External World.

That He was also attested by His own Perfection, which would have lacked (and, therefore, not existed) had He yielded to human force and failed to fulfil His Work, even at the cost of torture and Death.

Moreover that not undergoing Death He could not

give the crowning evidence of his Nature and Mission, and the highest guarantee of our hope—His Resurrection.

[It is believed that this fragment, found pencilled on a loose sheet of paper, between the leaves of a note-book containing exclusively religious memoranda, was one of many attempts made by Mr. Dobell to draw up (in what to himself should appear a satisfactory form) a 'neutral' or 'negative' creed. To the desirability of such a Creed allusion is several times made, as will have been seen, in the course of these 'Notes and Memoranda.'—ED.]

ETHICAL.

See this small beetle feeling its way with *palpi.*—So I 'feel after, if haply I may find,' through the unseen of Truth : so tardily, warily, in doubt—suspecting, trying, re-trying, turning, retrograding, progressing.

[From notes and memoranda concerning 'Philosopher' of the Drama.]

It may be argued in defence of Religious fallacies that God Himself sanctions the principle involved in them by never permitting us to know absolute Truth.

May it not be answered to this that those phenomena which we are compelled to take for truths all bear relations to Truth absolute, and, however apparently diverse from it, are but versions, in various tongues, of the same original, dilutions, more or less rare, of the same essence.

But not so with the artifices and mistakes of Mankind.

Religion the humanization of God. In order to a

correct humanization, a standard necessary, and a living standard—hence Immanuel.

Christ manifests in flesh and blood all attributes that Man can positively know, and leaves the remaining Deity to the infinite and immaterial suggestions of negatives.

The various ascetic and similar errors of Mankind have arisen from an ignorance that the object of Religion is the attainment of ideal *Humanity*—not the super-human, if such there be among finite Beings.

Love of God and love of our neighbour. As we see in a grain of corn that sends down a life earthward, which we call the root, and sends up a life Heavenward, which we call leaf and flower, both lives being the same being, so perhaps the love of our neighbour is but a mode of the love of God.

Sin, in action, is that action which either indicates the activity of mental qualities that should be inactive, or the inactivity of such as should be active.

'Abstain from every shape of evil,'—*i.e.* from evil in every shape, even though it take the form of an 'Angel of Light.'

Whether good should be welcomed even if coming in horns and cloven hoofs—*i.e.* actions essentially good should take place irrespective of appearances—must be decided by the force of controlling principles on the merits of each case.

In the daily casuistries of conscience there is a right, as high as most of those with which they are conversant, that is too frequently forgotten.

It is the right of each member of the Cosmos of Human Duties to its share—and its *proportionate* share— of the limited sum total of each man's vital energy.

When that share has been spent on the given *vexata questio* no more can be given without a moral fraud upon other problems.

('*Piety*.') The God of every man is modified by his own nature—in many men has no existence but in themselves. There may be cases, therefore, in which the more pious a man the worse his morality.

HAPPINESS AND PLEASURE.

If one defines happiness as the pleasure of all such moral functions as have more than terrestrial fields of action is it not to say the pleasure of Love—for which other has more than mortal scope?

But to limit true happiness to the exercise of those immortal functions is to produce in the mortal man a partial and fragmentary activity, and to discourage corporate and harmonious life.

Yet we say that self-sacrifice, the denial of 'pleasure' *et hoc genus* is the means of true happiness. But is not this because thus we make that internal *quasi*-silence in which alone, in most men, as yet, the pleasure of the higher functions can be heard? And because herein we have the readiest means of exercise (exercise being necessary to pleasure) for some of those functions which do not readily find objects of use?

Is not Happiness rather the harmonious pleasure of all the functions in their ideal proportions?

———

Fully to understand moral principles and their application it is necessary to realize a chaotic state of pancratic, or other, aboriginal society, and to realize their action there.

This applies to moral principles and qualities whencever their origin. See how the good man must needs act under these conditions. The truths deducible from that experiment serve as a body for the subtler soul of the moral theory and practice of a hypercivilized time.

The nature of the virtues is such that, though each does not the function of the other, those things which are most consistent with all are specifically most congruous with each.

Goodness is the highest terrestrial Beauty of which we know, because Goodness is Beauty expressed in the highest terrestrial substance of which we know—*i.e.* Human Nature.

There is a certain familiarity with sacred things which may arise from the very completeness of reverence. *Mens sibi conscia* of a veneration beyond suspicion will allow itself a lightness which to the careless eye looks like the result of opposite causes.

Was not Neoplatonism the result of a new cerebral excitement introduced from the East and till then unknown?

The phenomena of ecstasy &c., may be accounted for by the fact that the faculty of the brain by which it prays and venerates is of more endurance in some natures than the other faculties and still vibrates when they are enfeebled past action.

TWO VIEWS OF SOCIAL DUTY.

One: 'resist not evil,' give up the good and beautiful to the evil and ugly and thus, as it were, force the Divine Interposition of a miraculous government of this World.

The other: let the social conscience make itself objective in laws and their consequences, for the sake of those to whom personal conscience is insufficient; and by a terrestrial and present (necessarily gross and material) imitation of a celestial and future, supply for common natures the defect of imagination.

PRIEST.

The office of Priest has been, in all ages and peoples, to offer sacrifice—*i.e.* expiation, compensation (so to speak)—(that which pays the debt and releases the debtor, by a loss on his part, and atones him) and to pronounce absolution—*i.e.* this release.

If the two have not always gone together *in formâ*, they have done so implicitly by irresistible logic.

It is by this office of pronouncing absolution that they are the strongest and most terrible tyrants of mankind; and it is by the absence of this that the clergy of the English Churches cease to be priests or tyrants and merely rank with other machineries, more or less useful for enlightenment.

PROPHET.

He whose ear and eye (the finer ear), external and internal, are able to receive and to repeat voices within and without : *i.e.*

I. To perceive the agreement of facts and processes not-human with human facts and processes, or with facts and processes possible to the limited mind of man, and therefore communicable, by some means, from man to man.

II. To experience in reaction to some not-human fact or system of facts some new sensation or notion, congruous with it, and communicable.

It might be theorized that a hierarchy of Priests, depositaries of recognized Truth, and censors of new utterances, might be the right corrective of Prophets.

But who have killed the Prophets; who slew the Holy and the Just and desired a murderer?

Not the 'common people,' not the civil power, but they who followed Caiphas.

THE EVIL OF A PRIESTHOOD.

Christianity gives Ideas and Principles as perceptible to the perfect human mind—as Divinely revealed—to be rendered into practice by the imperfect human mind, *selon son possible*.

The evil of a Priesthood is that it must make one of two mistakes—must impose on the imperfect the practice congruous with the perfect, or must think down to the imperfect. Either mistake equally fatal to the subtlest values and processes of Christianity. A Man who would judge men must live the life of men. Otherwise he no longer sees human facts as they are. The blood no longer in the flesh what is it but dust? Therefore to Priestly eyes the passions of Mankind cannot be seen truly. The precaution taken to secure truth makes truth impossible.

— — —

The immense danger of symbolical forms or ceremonies is that they may be misunderstood for what they symbolize. The further the symbol deviates from true metaphor the more mortal this danger.

Vide Egyptian hieroglyphs and the Mexican worship: in the latter note the sacrifice of *living hearts*.

The ready reception of mythological solutions illustrates the action of instinct in the imperfect human nature.

A heap of stones is found on a hill. The instinct that asks a cause for every effect becomes active. But when tradition declares that the devil threw them from the opposite hill the satisfied instinct is at rest.

DEMONOLOGY.

We think our science disproves demonology by assigning the nature and succession of facts called by scientific names.

But how if we be but anatomizing not disproving it?

Therefore the ancients said of such intelligences that they had three names—for earthly, Heavenly, and infernal use.

Quoad foregoing.

If we use 'Law' (of Nature) in the sense of a formula of Will, only, demonology is the inevitable consequence, for that which is *conscious* and obedient is an intelligence.

If we use 'Law' for *Ordo*—a formula of performance, only, then the Sole Doer is responsible for all facts.

WAR.

Memoranda of facts aiding towards enquiry if it can be Christian.

The principle 'Do unto others' does not militate against it, inasmuch as I respect the antagonist for doing to me what I intend to do to him.

Both parties meet under an implied permission to destroy.

But the permission of a co-agent with regard to actions *quoad se* does not necessarily make them lawful—*e.g.* fornication.

The permission of the *Patiens*, however, legalizes any action not culpable *per se—i.e.* not expressing a quality that should be silent or evidencing the silence of one that should be expressed—*e.g.* amputation.

The question therefore of whether War can be Christian turns on the qualities which it necessarily expresses? Not the qualities that are usually expressed by it but those without the action of which it *cannot take place*?

A Christian's action must usually indicate the mean resulting force of various qualities. The application of one Principle is always open to the modifying power of another Principle.

'Render to no man evil for evil.' But evil depends not on the action but the quality expressed by it. To cut off my neighbour's arm in hate is evil. To do so in love is surgery. (The second clause, 'but contrariwise blessing,' is in complete keeping with this deeper interpretation of evil.)

'Love your enemies. Do good to them that hate you.' The first clause is the principle of which the second is one application. That application presupposes the proper time and place. There are circumstances to which it is impossible it can apply—because no specific kind of action can be incessant—other duties counteracting. *Ergo* it is not universal. If not universal then to be applied according to circumstances.

What if I remember my duties to my enemies at the time proper to those to my friends?

On what principle do we act in meeting the other difficulties of life? Is it by prayer and trust *without* action or prayer and trust *upon* action? And surely the Christian *modus operandi* should be consistent under all circumstances.

Violence to the soul is admitted, on all sides, to be occasionally justifiable (Rebuke, &c. &c.) Is it possible that violence to the body can be worse?

Since in the Mosaic Dispensation we know that

Warriors were 'after God's own heart' there must, if War is now unlawful, be some *Differentia* of Christianity which makes it so. That difference is usually supposed to be contained in the sayings commencing 'it hath been said of old time thou shalt love thy neighbour and *hate* thine enemy'—'an eye for an eye, a tooth for a tooth.' But, carefully examined, are not these purely applicable to *vengeance*? And no more relative to 'War' than to 'Peace?' It is not the prevention of violence by violence but the *punishment* of successful violence that the illustration exposes, and the principle 'hate thine enemy' concords with the illustration. Surely a *Differentia* more unmistakeable is required to set aside the precedent of Abraham, Moses, Joshua, and David.

Hate seeks the injury of the object *as an end*. By whatsoever *means* (however pleasant) such end unlawful.

'Your powers are given you for the benefit never the injury of others.' But may I not benefit through pain—*e.g.* surgery? 'Yes, but that is pain for the benefit of the sufferer.' But if I may lawfully so benefit this wretch who for a shilling to drink with is trying to murder me, may I not yet more virtuously benefit *through his pain* those lovely and good beings whose welfare depends on mine?

'Do unto others as you would have them do to you'— *i.e.* as you being you would have them do to you *if you* were they. If I—being what I now am—were doing to me what my murderer is doing I would wish that he should make the stoutest resistance possible. Therefore if a murderer attacks me I should make such resistance.

'Love your enemies'—*i.e.* love *even* your enemies.

Let your Sun of love be so warm and light that having heated and lit its solar system a large nebula of superabundant light califies the cold dark beyond.

'If you love them that love you what thank have ye'— for you must be below the beasts to do less. *Humanity excels the brutes in those things wherein brutes are virtuous; and Christian humanity is conterminous with the perfection of the natural human virtues, beginning* at their culmination.

With what a love shall he love his friends who is able to love even his enemies! This is Christianity in accordance whereto says St. Paul 'do good to all—specially to the household of Faith.'

He who loves his enemies without loving his friends is not Christianized but diseased.

We find it difficult to love our enemy from a fault rather of perception than of feeling.

If we truly *perceived* the Being in the midst of distorted passions, &c. we should pulse with such an emotion as at seeing a victim in the flames, or an animal agonizing in the toils.

POLITICAL

PAMPHLET ON REFORM.[1]

>   England;
> That holy island of the temperate seas
> Where Man and Nature keep the sweet degrees
> Of modest seasons, that in mild advance
> Measure with changing step the time and dance
> Of sacred Order, ever new and old.   .   .

MY DEAR FRIEND,—You wish me to set forth in a Pamphlet-letter the scheme of enfranchisement to which I alluded in our late conversation on Parliamentary Reform. Even your flattering request would not compel me to what must necessarily be a brief and insufficient exposition of that scheme, if I did not care more for its principles than for the machinery by which I propose to apply them; and if I did not believe that the question of Reform will retain its troublesome Premier-haunting character, till we answer it on principles more organic, expressed in machinery more natural, than those of that provisional

---

[1] The first edition of this Pamphlet was published in 1865.

and temporary reply which in 1832, was the best that state exigencies allowed.

I am the less willing to wait for greater leisure to either of us, because a great national controversy on the subject of Reform seems presaged pretty plainly for the coming year; and as Parliamentary Reform has come in our day to mean reform of the popular branch of Parliament, and the patient is not usually the best judge of his own case, one is glad to expect that, in this age of journalism, a large part of the discussion will be outside the House of Commons.

But if Parliament has special difficulties in discussing Parliamentary Reform, arising from the retrospective self-conscious character of the investigation, the non-parliamentary world has also special difficulties, resulting from an opposite cause. If the legislature, with its eyes turned inward, is unlikely to get a just notion of its own objective personality, we who regard it from without are too much impressed with the characteristics of its bodily presence. And that bodily presence is, at this point in our history, precisely of the kind on which it is most dangerous to reason, because it assumes and has assumed for more than thirty years (that is to say, during the political life of those who will be most likely to examine it) the shape of a hybrid. A hybrid, as most of us are aware, may be very safe and useful in action, but it is singularly untractable and misleading as an object of scientific enquiry, especially when that inquiry is for the discovery of organic principles.

As we all know, the Parliament of England was, up to times quite recent, a means of assisting a governing sovereign, or a governing oligarchy, with what wisdom might be in the nation; and the theory of parliamentary representation, as understood by our earlier jurists, was the rationale of a method for eliminating that wisdom and presenting it to the ruler. When, however, in process of time the sovereign reigned without governing, when England, gradually and unconsciously, became the only safe republic that ever existed (because a republic wherein the highest prize in social rank is impossible to the ambition of any citizen), Parliament virtually assumed to be the *alter ego* of the governing nation, and by parliamentary representation the nation sought to epitomize itself in microcosm.

But as this change in the problem, and in the desideratum, was never theoretically stated, and as (faithful to that peculiarity in all our English changes by which we avoid the break of continuity that is mortal to all, except the lowest, living bodies) the modern Parliament and the ancient Parliament differed little in appearance and materials, it was natural that many observers should ignore what had essentially taken place. We had turned the old wisdom-making machine into a kind of demometer, but the two natures refused to mix; we had compounded without transubstantiation. Therefore, while the popular politician honestly discerns in the resulting institution only one modern version of democracy, the conservative eye as honestly perceives only the last form of 'Witena Gemot.' According to the Witena-gemotic system, the principles on which Parliament should, if needful, be further modified, would seem, at first glance, to be simple. Whenever a non-electing class in the nation can demonstrate its share in whatever qualities are expressed by 'Witena' in equal degree with any class already possessing the electoral franchise, that non-electing class has proved its right to share the possession. But further consideration will show that this simple formula is not sufficient to the practical case where every accession of numbers is apt to consist mainly of those possessing a minimum of the qualifications. Now to increase the number of inferior choosers is, of course, where majorities are to decide, to deteriorate the chances of the choice. But who will ever convince the excluded class of the justice of their exclusion? Or who can wonder that the denial of claims which, to the claimants, must appear irresistible, arouse those heartburnings which, when inflaming great masses of physical force, end in rebellion and revolution? I will not pause upon these and other difficulties, in any theory of parliamentary representation that has '*wisdom*,' in the popular sense, for its final cause, because we have to seek in our modern Parliament rather those vital principles by which it may subserve present and future necessities than those by which, however beautifully and beneficially, it connects the present with the past.

By the 'Reform Act,' and by the Parliamentary policy that has succeeded it, we practically gave up the advantages of being governed by others wiser than ourselves (as under our original Parliaments) for certain other advantages supposed to result from *self-government*. But the amount of advantage from self-government—whether individual or national—is in proportion to its genuine thoroughness. Experience shows that the mistakes and ill-doings of self-government are, in the long run, more advantageous to the governed, because more conducive to real progress, than the sage anachronisms and out-of-place wisdom of governors whose mental and moral rank is, for other purposes, far superior to their own. But for the errors of self-government to be salutary they must be genuine: for the sins we commit under partial compulsion have little, if any, therapeutic effect upon us; and good deeds mechanically done are nearly useless to moral development.

By partial self-government we lose, at once, the specific advantages of nationality and bureaucracy—the educational effects of our own right and wrong, and the temporary and superficial benefits which might accrue from a perfunctory subservience to others. It seems to me therefore that, in endeavouring to represent the British people in Parliament, you must, at the stage of national life to which we are arrived, endeavour towards whatever may (in the truest, completest, and most living manner) realize self-government;—whatever will, in such time and place as is consistent with unity of action, represent that British nation which, in a manner inconsistent with such unity, is spread abroad over these islands.

Now, in representing an individual, whether man or nation, so that it may virtually be and act, *en permanence*, in a place where it is not, how must you represent it? Neither at its best nor its worst; but at the best which it can healthily and continuously maintain. Represent a man in that state wherein he says his prayers, or makes love, or reads poetry, or enjoys fine pictures, or performs an heroic action, and your representation is, for practical purposes, untrue; because no man can healthily maintain himself in that key through all the hours of every day. Represent his lowest possibilities, and you are still more perniciously false. Represent him even at a vulgar mean, below what his qualities can healthily, harmoniously, and continuously reach, and your representation, if he is bound to realize it (and parliamentary representation is, as we have seen, a representation we are bound to realize), is untrue, and morally deleterious. But represent him at the highest moral, intellectual, spiritual, and physical degree, which, with no more strain than is healthy stimulus, he can consistently and effectively maintain, and your representation, being true to the essential and persistent characteristics of the original, will not only represent him fairly, honestly, and efficiently to others, but, if he is to back it by personal action, will place himself under exactly those fortunate conditions of present exercise which are also the happiest guarantees of beneficial development. If these things be true of just representation when the individual to be represented is a man, they will be found, I think, equally true when the original to be reproduced is that large man a nation. I assume, therefore, that a just national representation is such as represents the nation AT ITS EFFICIENT DURABLE BEST. Granted this kind of representation to be desirable, by what machinery can it be accomplished? Not by such as should merely represent numbers; for numbers, inspired by something that is not due to number, are capable of a higher national life than they could themselves originate. These flesh and bones of the state depend, and seem likely long to depend, for their noblest national character, on the vital life supplied by other functions. Yet numbers must not be unrepresented. You cannot appraise a man's total nature by his bodily weight and forces, but in representing his sum of ability you omit them at your peril. Nor, for similar, but not identical, reasons, is it sufficient to represent property. We want not a democracy—in the modern sense—nor a plutocracy, but a nation: and not only a nation, but, as I have already suggested, a nation at its efficient durable best. Extremes are comparatively easy, and so is vulgar mediocrity; but the healthy best has always been the crucial difficulty of portrait-painter, moralist, and psychologist. And if to create this kind of other-he is difficult when the primary self is an individual man, how much more difficult when it is a nation!

I think there are four obvious methods in which, with more or less success, it might be attempted. (1) One, but the least desirable, would be to represent classes instead of places. You might so represent classes as to create an assembly of intensely typical men, whose correlation of forces might result in such a dynamical mean as should give the strength and direction of thinking and feeling England. The highest philosophy, the merest heroism, the widest knowledge, might leaven the grosser representatives of the (so to speak) popular flesh and blood, to a total that should express the nation at its 'efficient durable best.' But, apart from the fact of our instinctive English dislike to class representations, by adopting this mode we should be guilty of a great waste of mental power. We do not want philosophers in the legislature. Their function is to prepare governors and governed for a better than the present best; and their legislation would always, therefore, be that most pathetic kind of failure, the impractability of beautiful anachronism. Discarding this method, I see three others. (2) You might endeavour so to modify the franchise as to favour a practical union of all the aristocracies—the aristocracy of blood, of talent, of land, of wealth, of science, and of skill—*e.g.* the hereditary 'nobility and gentry,' the chief thinkers, artists and learners, the exceptional traders, and the skilled artisans, against the dead weight of mere numbers and stupid welfare. (3) Or you might, by slightly altering our present modes, make a Parliament of political physicians, able in popular diagnosis, who should do as a legislature what journalism does in another fashion—

reproduce, to the best of their power, that which tact, talent, and study teach them to be 'Public opinion.' (4) Or you might create a self-adjusting electoral machine to do that work in a less conscious and voluntary manner. Of the second and third of these methods I say nothing here, except that I would rather not depend on them till the fourth has proved impossible. And of the self-adjusting self-registering machinery for that fourth? Towards some mechanism of this sort I would, with much diffidence, offer the following suggestions :—

The thing of which you would create such another self as you can bring into the palace of Westminster, is not a nomadic or stationary crowd, but that unity a nation. Therefore, in representing its constituent parts, you must represent them in their constituent character. That is to say, in representing the proportionate value of each constituent, you must estimate his part in the size, shape, and weight of that unity, his formative share in the national whole;—*i.e.* you must represent him not as the man but as the citizen. This large One a nation, is, so to speak, a great Chinese puzzle, made up of different parts, each part differing in size and shape; and in estimating the political value of a man, you require to know not what and how much he is, *per se*, but what and how much of him goes to the puzzle. You are going to make an enormous national *civis*, and you must make it by aggregating not men but citizens. *You must, therefore, give to each voter who co-acts with his fellow-citizens in choosing a representative, such an amount of influence in that choice as shall express his comparative value as a citizen.* The special characteristics of a citizen are, I think, those which relate him to his compatriots (including in that term his sovereign and his fellow-citizens) and those which relate him to a certain quantity of the earth and its goods—social relations and 'vested interests.' If it is answered that, inasmuch as relations may exist without corresponding virtues, and interests without adequate rights, the representation of relations and interests would not necessarily reach our standard of 'efficient durable best' I would reply that, in the present state of our laws, and of their administration, *the maintenance of interests and relations is, taken generally and for practical purposes, sufficient proof and measure of the virtues that should actuate and the rights that should justify them, e.g.* that out of a given number of masters and heads of families there will be a large majority in whom those relations indicate the presence of an average amount of the appropriate magisterial and paternal qualities. Therefore, if you represent social relations and vested interests, you are not only representing the outward configuration of the citizen, his civic size, shape, and weight, and consequently his constructional value in the national form, but you also represent, in as accurate a way as is usually possible to great human estimates, the virtues and the rights which are his quota in the total heart, soul, and conscience, of the living body-politic. Which of the social relations should represent themselves—which of a man's social conditions as subject, husband, father, master, servant, artisan, tradesman, ratepayer, landlord, tenant, dealer, capitalist, graduate in-arts, and the like, should separately represent itself by an electoral vote, and should therefore add to that sum of votes by which I would express his comparative importance as a citizen, is a matter of detail that may be left to another time and place. But I would indicate a distinction between relations and interests, which seems of vital moment. Objectors demur to the enfranchisement of interests, on the plea that (inasmuch as interests always involve relations)—'property has its duties as well as its rights'— to enfranchise an interest, *in se*, would be to give an undue preponderance to property. *Social Relations* should be counted in estimating the citizen as a component part of the state, because each new social office which a man fills binds him to his fellows by a new kind of social obligation. It is the kind and not the quantity of the obligation that the relation expresses, and, in the majority of cases, it is the kind rather than the quantity that affects his value and character as a citizen. A man with his third wife may be no more husbandly than with his first; and the fathers of a dozen children and of one may be equally paternal. But when we come to deal with *Interests*, expressing rights, the case is different, because it is not so much the kind as, so to speak, the quantity of right that expresses a man's shape and weight as a citizen. That the widow's mite when she gives it up to the state may represent as much patriotism as the million pounds of the millionaire is quite true ; but in this it is the measure of a virtue and not of a right ;—and a measure so difficult of use and gauge as to be unavailable for the rough purposes of human government. Every man not a felon or a pauper has, viewed as a subject for legislation, a dual existence— he exists *per se*, and by the proxy of his goods. Legislation cannot move without impinging on goods ; but as it never affects them as possessions of tenants in common, or as a copartnery of equal shares, the size of that second existence is a quantity differing in every citizen. A statute that impartially levies so much in the hypothetical pound practically means that, though I and my neighbour look so much alike, I am to pay a trifle and he is to bleed thousands a year, but it it evident that my neighbour's real personality is, as regards this law, greater than mine. While, therefore, the real self of one man so differs from that of another, self-government requires a representative expression of that difference; whether that difference consist in the differing number of functions whereby a man assists in composing that total citizen the state, or in the differing size of his share in that great partnership, whereby this political corporation holds its lands and goods. *And those who propose to find that expression in a plurality of votes, are only adopting, for parliamentary elections, a machinery which, in regard to the smaller elections for parochial parliaments, has already the assent of the country.* The idea of plural voting has been recognized in English political life from time immemorial, and the facts that some districts return one and some two members to Parliament—*i.e.* that each elector in the one has double the choosing power of his compatriot in the other—and that the same elector may have a vote for more than one locality—*i.e.* that as concerns the result of an election his power may be multiplied to any extent of which locomotion will allow—so far nullify the entire electoral equality that has been claimed for the present system as to throw doubt on its fundamental character. I am aware of the objections which will spring to the imagination of many politicians, when I propose that *the vote of every British subject, unconvicted of crime, shall be taken at the elections of members to serve in Parliament, but shall be reckoned* (according to some scale to be fixed after due parliamentary inquiry) *at a value commensurate with the number of his social relations and the extent of his rights of property* :— counting one for the man, if any such exist, who is only a subject, and so on, upwards, for every other qualification.

That is to say, I would propose that the total of votes at a general election should represent the total of civic functions that make up that vast *civis* the nation, and the total of lands and goods which he rightfully possesses; and that the number of these votes given by any one *civiculus* (so to speak) should indicate the value of him and his in the composition of those national wholes. Believing that a plan of this kind is likely to secure the end I have ventured to propose as the object of all beneficial representation—the representation of the thing represented 'at its efficient durable best'—I would beg the further patience of yourself and your friends while I point out some other advantages which seem to inhere in such a system.

1. To ascertain the electoral qualifications of an

elector would require no new or inquisitorial machinery. As I propose to enfranchise not moral or intellectual qualities, but the civic functions which, on the average (and an average quite as high as that of the political ability indicated by tenancy of a 10*l.* house), are their social signs, not abstract rights, but those possessions which, when unquestioned by the law, are their sufficiently accurate evidence, the new franchise would have to take cognizance of nothing that was not already recognized and identified by title-deeds, diplomas, tax-receipts, licences, parish-registers, apprenticeship-indentures, and the like unmistakable testimony. It is not amenable, therefore, to the strong arguments that have been urged against a metaphysical franchise.

2. As comprehensive and self-adjusting, it would be likely to save us from those eras of organic change which, viewed from within or without, have hitherto been the great perils of constitutional peoples. Making the *personnel* of the constitution commensurate with the nation, you rest it on that immoveable basis of the earth whereon terrestrial things can alone be permanent, instead of poising it on a seething mass of incongruous life,—like those carved Italian pulpits whose supports are running beasts and fighting men. By such a system, the passage of the 'lowest' classes in the State to great

political power would happen, without convulsion or organic strain, in proportion as they added to their numerical force those civic functions which raise them in the scale of virtual citizenship,—that is to say, in proportion as they became part of the nation's 'efficient durable best.'

3. It would save us from universal suffrage, popularly so called. To resist that most mortal of all enemies to human progress without denying any claims that can, by proving themselves consistent with that progress, show presumptive proofs that they are rights, is surely among the first present duties of British statesmanship. By enfranchising every non-criminal British subject, and ending that indefinite consciousness of half-understood wrong which must exist in every man whose political existence is denied, you relieve the State for ever from a great chronic danger which any lassitude or incompetence in those who, from time to time, adjust the political safety-valves, may convert into the most active maleficent force. 'Universal suffrage'—the plan, *i.e.* of ringing up the servants to settle your vexed questions of philosophy, art, and morals—has too little attraction for the English order of mind to be ever an indigenous danger; but as it is in full force in nations with whom every day is bringing us into more sympathetic union, we

are likely, without preventive care, to receive, by infection, a disease not congenital to British common sense. For that preventive care no mere theoretical demonstration will suffice. To convince the reason that 'universal suffrage' is unreasonable will be useless, so far as the excluded classes are concerned, while feeling answers that its denial involves the refusal of a right, and its establishment the removal of a wrong. To show that what is called 'universal suffrage' is not 'universal' at all (since the suffrage of the beaten minority is not represented in the result), but really means absolute choice by whatever party happens to be the most numerous; that, in the present (and every other immature) state of the world, the condition of mind which chooses ill, under difficulties, is more common than the condition which chooses well; that therefore, when mere numbers choose, their choice (deducting for exceptions) will be erroneous; that the knowledge of this will deter the best men from offering themselves to electors who are known to prefer the inferior; to show that an assembly, from which the better elements had been eliminated or in which their influence was hopelessly overborne, so far from realizing that 'efficient durable best' which is the necessary condition of collective progress, must degrade its own individuality and, withdrawing it more and more from partnership in the community of peoples,—eventually make its political existence a menace to the civilized world; to show all this, and conclude that such an electoral system is one of the most preposterous mistakes and deceptions by which the half-thinking of sentimental or passionate theorists, and the policy or profligacy of astute or desperate adventurers, ever caught the multitude, will avail nothing to convince that very multitude, while the grievance of an exclusion, which no reasoning can disprove, is agitating their passions by the ignominy of odious comparison. Nor will it avail much more to point across the Atlantic, where, with a thousand exceptional conditions to favour the experiment, the system, even thus early in the national history, has notoriously shut out the best minds of America from politics, and set nearly every tuning-fork of public opinion to the lower key-notes of the country: nor across the Channel, where, with whatever apparent temporary success, the worst evils of the machine are corrected by Imperial interference, and to show that this mode of amendment is as faulty in principle as we know it to be demoralising in practice. If, in the countries of universal suffrage, the heads of the State are not such men as universal suffrage would naturally select, they have, by their own hypothesis, no right to govern. If, on the other hand, they are truly the exponents of that suffrage, their interference in the further action of the electoral machine merely completes the vicious circle of that pernicious consistency whereby the higher arc of the national whole is perpetually wheeling under, and the upward shoots of popular life are continually contorted towards the ground. In such a State the virtues and abilities which are the natural captains of progress are incessantly reduced to the ranks, and the nation which, by encouraging what is best, highest, and most beautiful within it, should be a vast school of human and national advancement, is converted (by deliberately making a goal of zero, a lesson of ignorance, and a standard of '*ipsissimum vulgus*,') into an enormous engine of personal, social, and political retrogression.

These *argumenta ad homines* are useless, because they appeal to precisely that knowledge of human character, and to that political wisdom, which the classes addressed are certain not to possess. To the ploughman, the difference in statesmanship between Lord Palmerston and Mr. Stanton is inappreciable; but he perceives quite well, that while he had no vote for the one, any ploughman in America might have voted for the other.

By representing every man's comparative weight in the state, instead of enfranchising a mere unit of number,

I believe that you would satisfy whatever may be just in the claims of numbers as numbers, while you counteract the possibility of a numerical despotism; and you, therefore, attain the advantages of universal suffrage without those evils by which it has been the bane of politics, and which must rank it as an electoral system—whether such system be considered as an engine of present welfare or as a progress-machine—among the least rational adaptations of means to ends, by which those semi-passions that so often pass for reason have humoured the desires, apologized for the foregone conclusions, and hocused the conscience of mankind.

4. It is favourable to hereditary monarchy. By the polarity of things, democracy—when it means the rule of the multitude—must always be liable to Cæsarism, and that Cæsarism may virtually include the four-year king, called president, late American events have suggested. I need not here go into the argument by which it would be easy to prove that *elective* monarchy—called by whatever name—is as incompatible with the political machinery of a true republic as it is injurious to the moral, spiritual, and artistic life of the people who create it; and that the only royalty which consists with the necessities of constitutional freedom is a function of the body-politic too fine to be made and remade periodically by the rude

hands of voting millions. That positive of so many negations, that aureole of reflex rays and refracted colours, that cerebral plexus of converging and reverting nerves and forces, is impossible to the turbulence of popular change; only in the unshaken quiet of absolute security can the undisturbed elements take the fortunate concurrence. But though the argument for hereditary monarchy is so well understood in England that I may assume its conclusions for granted, it may be well to point out that hereditary monarchy, to be a political success, must find among the people consistent habits of thought and congruous social institutions. If not, the gilded car of royalty ballooning in mid-air above the levels of 'Liberté, Egalité,' will become an idol or a popinjay; or the king, standing in midst of those levels, will soon, since a king's stature is not necessarily greater than a subject's, be run down by the contempt of multitudinous familiarity. In other words, royalty in the one case, too far removed from the common people to be the object of useful criticism, and surrounding itself—since kings are men, and have men's necessities of love and friendship—with a self-created cabal of favourites, would become a peril to liberty, or an exasperating mark for popular passions: in the other case, the exigencies of daily life would so vulgarise the king and his function, that the idea of the function would be lost in that of the man—a loss mortal to hereditary rule unless in those exceptional kingdoms founded, so to speak, by demigods, whose superhuman longevity is represented by their heirs. The present French empire is an instance of this rare kind, and should never be counted among elective monarchies. You remember the guardsman's answer to the news that the first Napoleon was dead,—' Lui mort! vous le connaissez bien!' That touching answer, unsurpassed in history, was really the answer of France. It was as vicegerent of this unconquerable immortality that Louis Napoleon came to power, the patent by which he took it was signed and dated in St. Helena.

In ordinary kingdoms, it is the monarchy rather than the monarch that is, and ought to be perennial; and that part of the popular imagination which conceives general notions has so little native force, that it requires to be protected from the competition of those keen personal images which, though they may occasionally dignify the ideas they represent, may also degrade or supersede them. I believe that some such electoral system as that which I have ventured to propose would favour among the people those habits of thought and that social attitude which would furnish a new safeguard to the great monarchical abstraction. By associating with the *popular notion of progress* the notion of *constitutional permanence*, and with the popular idea of liberty and civic fraternity the idea of *personal and political inequality*, and by creating among citizens the recognition and the exercise of a graduated order of power, I think it would prove not only the best expositor of popular rights, but would tend also to conserve that hereditary royalty without which (or its yet unknown substitute) no true republic can long exist.

5. It is at once Protestant and Catholic, and a guarantee, therefore, against the extension of Roman Catholic influence. Protestantism, of all varieties, must always rely upon the thinking and half-thinking classes; while, if the papacy is to exist, its future strength must be the millions. It must always rule through the very high or the very low. It is too well read to believe immediately that new facts are endurable; but when changes evidently irresistible show that power is never more to be won from the fears and hopes of a king, it will try the other pole of the same magnet and find it in the depths of the people. Hitherto its political strategy has been the mastery of an exceptional few of peculiar position, education, and resulting character, whose royal desire for the privilege of sinning safely, and known ability to pay for it royally, made them the special customers of 'St. Peter.' Henceforth the one prince is

carved into ten or twenty million; and since, in the nature of things, a like entourage of cardinals, bishops, confessors, or what not, can no longer be spent in the reduction of each unit in this multitude, the deficiency in available force will suggest a change in the character of the campaign. Twenty cacciatori may hardly manage a tiger, but one may suffice for a whole parish of sparrows. By a change in the nature, not of the sportsman but of the game, and a slight corresponding modification in the weapons, the disposable power of the Roman hierarchy may still do immense execution. Prey, adequately weak however, can usually be found only among the least intelligent of mankind; but as in the countries of universal suffrage, these classes must, for the next half-century, have a vast majority, it is exactly they who will be the possessors of sovereign power. The *parti prêtre* will soon perceive that in those countries universal suffrage means the despotism of the masses, and that the despotism of the masses means the despotism of those by whom the masses are swayed; that is to say, that the problem of obtaining political influence there, is the problem of obtaining personal and individual influence over the most ignorant and least able men and women in them. That personal and individual influence, entirely independent of reason or virtue, the wise machinery of the

Romish Church precisely enables it to acquire, and its admirable adaptivity will soon devise some such further instruments of popularity as may enable it for a time to besiege its enemies with the very troops they had mustered for its destruction. It may be said that these considerations apply to the continents of Europe and America, but are foreign to British interests. Without pointing to Ireland as a fulcrum for any papal Archimedes, I would suggest that at the present era it may be wise to foreclose the possibilities of any class by which Romanism may exercise pressure upon Parliament. The Church of England will probably exist as a personality long after, through that irresistible endosmosis and exosmosis whereby her ablest thinkers are already assimilating her to the heterodoxy of the external world, her present creed has passed into the next forward stage of spiritual transformation. When Parliament, in due season, has to formularize that change, it will be of the gravest importance that its action be purely expository, and that no temporary exertions of a party should put an institution so powerful for good or evil, and so certain— from the stability of its wealth, honours, and influence— to rouse all sacred and mundane ambitions, out of harmony with 'the efficient durable best' of the nation to which it belongs.

6. It would give a higher sanction to the action of Government on minorities.

When we say that a nation electing its representatives by this or that kind of franchise would be self-governed, we mean, of course, that the dominating party or parties in it would be self-governed. However much you may attempt to 'represent minorities,' there must always be a residue of unrepresented nonconformity, who must submit to a government in the making of which they have had no direct share. Towards such minorities, whether large or small, the party or union of parties, which is politically, for the time being, the nation, acts as man to man. It may, therefore, be of the greatest importance that the title of the one to temporary empire should be such as commands the conscience of the other. In quiet times the more conventional and superficial considerations for which the loser submits to the winner (as, for instance, the compact to abide by the results of an appeal to numbers, which is implied by electoral coaction) are sufficient to insure the good-humour of the game; but in great crises it may be of vital consequence that the few thinkers who, in all parties, control the many workers, should be able to recognize more radical claims to respect. Now, in actions between individual men, an agent's highest claim to act is, that he acts in his moral right. The highest presumptive evidence that he is in his moral right is, therefore, the best available evidence of his title to act. That the proof of his title to act would not necessarily be proof of his title to act unopposed, may be very true; but if it immensely increases the gravamen and responsibilities of opposition, its political value is nearly as great. Now a nation acting by an organism that represents its efficient durable best, offers the highest presumptive evidence that it acts in its moral right; and comes therefore to a dissident minority, with the highest available title to empire.

Man is not an unreasoning creature, unconsciously developing and ignorantly realizing that 'relative good' by which he will attain perfection. He is a *mens sibi conscia recti*,—a self-conscious mind, not only doing and being good, but having ideas of it and of himself in relation to it. These ideas shape his moral right. The mental function concerned with them seems to be that plexus of abilities commonly called 'conscience.' This plexus seems to have two signal characteristics: the aptitude to receive moral ideas *ab extra*, whether as abstractions or as images; and the power to secern a mirage of them, when deprived of the natural object. Now education, anthropology, or howsoever you would name that branch of embryology, the science of developing-man, shows that in the diagnosis of his mental and moral progress there are some cardinal signs. Among these are: the content by the conscience of the highest notions of human perfection which it can, at the given time, honestly hold: the best conformity thereto which the remainder of his abilities can honestly, consistently, and healthily maintain. Turning from the science to the art of education, we may say, therefore, that these are the most favouring conditions of his good. A man is most likely to be relatively good and morally right when his powers and qualities are co-existing at their efficient durable best, and to establish that co-existence is to establish the highest probability of that good and right. Therefore, (granting that what is true for that human multiplicity in unity, the individual man, is true for that human multiplicity in unity, the individual nation), a people represented at its efficient durable best, and acting by that representation, offers to all challengers, and among others to any dissident minority that for the time may separate itself from the national whole, the highest attainable guarantee that it acts in its moral right, and, therefore, the most authoritative human claim to the respect of moral beings.

7. It offers the best securities to liberty. What is true liberty?

The being and doing of a perfect human being, whether man or nation, furnish the standard of absolute human good; relative human good is such being and doing as are, for the given creature, in the order of progress towards perfection. True liberty is the freedom for such being and doing. Now if, as we may safely take for granted, in a society of imperfect, perfectible beings, the relation of no two beings to perfection is exactly the same, the good of each must differ from that of his neighbour, and his liberty must therefore differ also. There may be those whose liberty is a freedom nearly absolute, and there may be those, on the other hand, whose truest liberty is little more than the freedom of willing not to be free. But if a million citizens have a million differing liberties, how are they to be harmonized? Organize the million, and apply to that complex human unit the organized million what you have found to be valid for that complex human unit the individual man. The million-fold unit may exact from the units which compose it what each of these units may exact from its constituents—just so much and no more subordination of the autonomy of each part as is necessary for the autonomy of the whole; *i.e.* just so much modification of its perfectionating order as a whole as may be necessary to 'perfectionate' it as a part; *i.e.* so much personal sacrifice in each of the million as may put the million-fold person in the order of its perfection, and may realize for it, therefore, the conditions of its moral good. Now we have found that any human being, man or nation, gives the highest presumptive evidence that he is in his perfectional order when he shows that he is and does at his efficient durable best. Therefore, a nation represented at its efficient durable best offers the highest proof that human fallibility permits of its right to control the personal liberty of every citizen who is a constituent of that representation. On such citizens as, not being represented, form part of a minority in such a state, I have already shown that the dominant majority have the highest attainable claims to respect. I think, therefore, I may fairly claim that, whether as regards the ruling majority or the dissentient minority, a nation so represented offers the highest guarantees for true constitutional liberty. Indeed may it not almost be said that a just realization of true liberty—*i.e.* of such relative liberty as is true to a given point in human progress—is only probable to a nation so organized: because no other nation is likely, as a nation, to have such ideas of right and wrong as are exactly congruous with its place in human history, or, dealing with events as they arise, could so completely embody or concentrate the unwritten law existing at the time and place in the given phase of the national conscience?

I believe that, in our own day, for example, we hardly guess how much such a people might safely simplify legislation, or how modest and sparse might be that well-placed and little-seen police of law, enforcing merely the primary and necessary conditions of all progress, by whose agency the great human concourse of moral liberties might march at all paces, in all measures, (in how many aberrations, and to what discordant tunes,) along the mighty highway of political freedom.

8. By representing property—*i.e.* by establishing a ratio between a man's legislative power and the extent of his liability to legislation—you subserve the principle of self-government, while by ballasting the restlessness of discontent with the salutary inertia of those who are satisfied, and exposing the cheap courage which risks the goods of others to the cautious censorship of self-interest, you make change sufficiently laborious to guarantee the safety of progress. And by thus giving a legal existence to the just influence of property, you starve out those illegal forms of political corruption by which at present it so balefully asserts itself, and which show such tenacity of

injurious life because they have root in one of those half-rights which no law dares authorize, but which no large justice can absolutely condemn. At the same time, by representing numbers, intelligence, and character, you insure us against 'Plutocracy'—which, as has been well said, is of all 'cracies' the most intolerable to a noble nation,—and provide us with a political body, which, while sufficiently coarse to incorporate, in good healthy workable bulk, the subtle forces of the national soul, and preserve us from the dangers of 'ideal' politics, shall be true to those organic principles whereby, in all living things whose arena is the earth, the obstruction of matter is informed with the immateriality of life, and finally, opened to the access and control of ideas.

9. By representing 'character' and 'intelligence,' you satisfy the cry for enfranchising intelligence and character; but by increasing the electoral value of each man in proportion as he is mental, moral, and serviceable, instead of endeavouring to give form and political activity to such abstractions as 'intelligence,' 'virtue,' or any other concept, you avoid the danger of creating monsters (for every human function or attribute dissected out from the rest, and invested with separate and active existence is monstrous) which must sooner or later evince their abnormity—as in historical precedents they have evinced

it—by preying on the wholesome complexities of natural life.

10. Combining the advantages without the dangers of democracy, oligarchy, and monarchy, we shall maintain that position by which it seems to be the vocation of our race to assist the education of mankind. Such an incarnation of an autonomy as, if not the final perfection of the creature, shall be a natural phase of the ordered change that culminates in perfection, should be the object of every one who, in any department of constructive art, endeavours to follow the Divine process of creation. Any nation realizing its 'efficient durable best' would certainly be such an incarnation; and whatever nation first achieved it would have the right, *de facto*, to expect a great formative influence on all the future political changes of the World. If that nation were British, the event would be additionally significant, because precisely one of those complementary facts that—like a half-discovered planet, guaranteed, while yet invisible, by the necessities of an extant solar system—complete the consistency of things already established. The more intimately we know the other tribes of civilized men, the more we must perceive that, though they are likely to excel us in particular functions of human genius, the special conditions of our origin and growth have given the body corporate of the British

people that truth to all manhood, that generic humanity of intense anthropomorphism (as opposed to the disembodied notions of speculators, or the characterless indifferentism of weak races), which fit it not only to expound the total progress of Europe, but to be the pivot-man, time-keeper, pitch-pipe, root-stem, or by whatever other metaphor from the arts you may express a living and dominating fact to which none of them have a precise analogue, of that slow universal transfiguration which is working out the destiny of man. By a self-sustaining, self-adapting, self-registering political organization, which shall amply, freely, and accurately give effect to our compound nationality, we shall best fulfil this splendid office, and best, therefore, insure that permanence therein whereby the system of nature rewards all special aptitudes. Qualifying ourselves for this proud position towards the world at large, by measures primarily taken with no ambition to that end, but honestly chosen for their supposed subservience to our most direct and personal duties, who knows that we may not unconsciously attain to the mysterious splendour of something even yet more sacred? The day may be far distant, and its supreme glory may not be for these latitudes, when a nation of perfect men and women, perfectly expressing itself, may be, the national Λόγος of social and political truth; but—as the clean hands and pure heart, even of men still imperfect, have before now dispensed the Divine Spirit—who shall say how soon, or how often, in the intervening future, a noble and Christian people, true, within and without, to its 'efficient durable best,' might utter by its legislation, and exemplify by its practice, a *vox populi* as yet unknown in the modern world—a voice that should prove the hackneyed adage to have been like many another bad proverb, the prophecy of those who, out of due time, perceived as accomplished fact the inevitable though it may be the distant goal.

Believe me, yours affectionately
SYDNEY DOBELL.

SOCIAL NOTES.

LAW.

The imagination of every time raises for itself a statue, expressed in Law, of a Righteous Man.

The law of the imperfect is that which in the individual and in the race shall advance it towards the perfect—*i.e.* which is educational in practice.

Action is language. Language has a certain value *per se* but is chiefly valuable for what it conveys: action is therefore important chiefly as expressing its (not final but) motive cause. In 'supplementing his imperfection' by Laws the imperfect therefore must deal primarily not with action but Agents. The imperfection to be supplemented is mental, and action must be controlled by Law with a primary view to mental results. Mental functions grow by *direct* exercise, therefore Law is not that which compels a simulacrum of the Perfect, but that which best stimulates and exercises the Principles of the Perfect in the Imperfect.

PROGRESS.

The fact that the whole humanity is necessary to the human Ideal by no means collides with the desire of progress in the scale of being, but is rather the condition of that progress, and the guarantee against such a destruction of balance as would make the disorganized progress *other* than true progress [in the scale of being].

No one can perceive (till the case reaches the extremes that are past cure) how, in a system of qualities so co-ordinated as the human, the advance of the *whole* is, by the mutual relations imposed on the constituents of it, the condition of the right advance of every *part*.

The various analogies by which the nature of Progress is expressed seem all liable to serious objection : 'development,' 'evolution,' beg the question : 'growth' is insufficient inasmuch as it may be fulfilled by increase of quantity, whereas all thinkers seem to mean by progress not merely a change from less than man can be to all that he can be, but a change under overruling conditions, such as would formerly have been expressed by the change of a being towards its 'final cause.'

'Progress,' in which the world professes to believe, seems to be a promorphosis or maturation of Mankind: (*i.e.* the breed of man, not necessarily the 'mankind' of any one era) : and as a corollary from this maturation of Man-the-Species, may be demonstrated the maturation of Man-the-individual, either by a change in existing individuals or in their progeny.

I am not bound to define progress, except in so far as that, by common consent, the word is to express some change in the Human Being, by which his present condition will be left behind that of the Man that shall be. If this is a change the Mankind and the Men that shall be will differ from the Mankind and the Men of now : if, as the world agrees, this change is desirable, we of to-day must be inferior to the future men ; if this maturing change is ever to reach an end the mature Man will be the perfect Man. And as one cannot think defect or excess in absolute Goodness, Truth, or Beauty, what he perceives will be True, what he is, feels, and does will be Good : *i.e.*, according to the sphere of existence or exercise, perfect Science, perfect Virtue, perfect Art.

But if the perfect Man has but attained to Truth and Goodness it follows that in the inferior states of mankind and men, what man perceives is erroneous, what he is, feels and does, sinful. And as, by common consent, the larger number of men are less mature than the exceptional few, it would seem that to put power in the hands of the many is to increase sin and falsehood.

But the majority of men desire to know truly, and desire either that themselves or their neighbours should be good: by common consent, therefore, it is desirable to hasten 'progress,' and the great problem, therefore, is to find what sorts of sin, error, and ugliness are in that order of which the final change is to goodness.

As Man the race is a convention of individual men, and as no programme of 'progress' completes it within the life of our generation, this problem requires an *examen* of change, as it occurs in Man the individual, and as it occurs in that succession of individuals, by which the race protends itself through 'Time.'

To examine how modern notions of government are or may be made consistent with progress notwithstanding the foregoing truths is one great object of this essay.[1]

ASSOCIATION.

There will always be many in a nation whose 'healthy durable best' is above and below the mean

---

[1] On 'the Physiology of Nations,' among notes for which the foregoing passages occur.—ED.

'healthy durable best' of the Nation. These should associate grade by grade. As the developing process of society elevates a member of each grade beyond the healthy permanent state of his fellows he should pass into the grade above. This developing process, acting on the unequally developable material of minds apparently similar, will create an inequality in the members of each grade long before the limits of corporate unity are passed. These unequal ascending-members are the natural leaders and teachers of their grade: and become afterwards the natural articulations of grade with grade.

Ideal Association. A number of ideal minds expressing themselves in action, ideal Society. Association being the necessary *méchanique* of human development Christianity as the ideal standard comes in the form of ideal association, not as demanding a specific Christian association but as furnishing the principles of all association.

REPRESENTATION.

What is representation? It is re-presentation—not in the sense of presenting the identical thing—the *corpus ipsissimum*—twice over—but, that thing being in one place, it is to present in another place such a copy—an *alter ego*—either on a larger or smaller scale, as shall have the same effect upon your mind—shall be to all intents and purposes the thing itself.

So we use the word in philosophy so in the practical concerns of life.

HOW SHALL A NATION BE REPRESENTED?

I. As it is. The representation should be a microcosm; a miniature. But how 'as it is'—for a nation, like an individual man, not only is, at any given epoch, but has phases of the same substantive existence?

Represent its best phase. Not what it may become, not its absolute ideal standard, but the best phase of its given positive degree of development. How is this to be distinguished? As in the case of the individual. That is the best phasis of the given state of an individual in which his noblest faculties are in as high, and his inferior faculties in as low, a state of activity as is consistent with HEALTHY PERMANENCE: *i.e.* with the permanence of those relations and the health of the Whole. Any such excitement as cannot be maintained may lead to reaction and incongruity; and any under-activity—*i.e.* below the healthy standard —may lead to dangerous accumulations of energy or to infective mortification.

So with the National Unit.

Let the noblest elements in a Nation—*e.g.* its intellect, morals, Devotion—have as much influence (and no more) and the lowest—*e.g.* Labour, (which till guided by the others is mere physique) as little (and no less), as fulfils the foregoing Law.

Let the National forces appear in the political microcosm not as they are potentially—*i.e.* as they would be if roused into the highest action of which each is capable—but as they should be decorously—*i.e.* in that state of relative excitement which may best conduce to the growth of the absolute National Ideal. What in Nations is 'self-government' subserves the same Law and therefore national self-government is always ill-favoured by high types of mind, because, the majority being always in a lower grade of development, the national application of principles is inconsistent with their application by those exceptional minds.

Such national application may also be inconsistent *temporarily* with apparent National Welfare, but is nevertheless always true to a higher welfare. Self-government therefore on the PRINCIPLES of *Ideal Society* is the nearest possible approach to Ideal Society. But self-government, except on those principles, is inevitable degradation. And as in the Individual the ideal principle should be applied by the best phasis of the then *status* of him, so in Society it should be applied by a large number of the Society's best Men, selected from the mass and by the mass *ad hoc.* For these men are to the Individual Society what his best phase is to the individual Man. But there is this difference—that in the individual Man all the qualities sympathetically share that total attitude which is his 'best phase:' whereas the lower elements of society are not in *rapport* with the best. Consequently even under these conditions Law is still untrue, and the only perfect government that by an angelic despotism, which could decide for each member of Society his special application of Principle.

MAJORITIES.

Why should Majorities govern? That they possess more wisdom than the few? But they have notoriously less. That, right or wrong, wise or foolish, they, as representing a larger modicum of the common will, and a larger portion of the surface whereon government acts, have claim to a proportionate *quantum* of power?

They—Majorities—might have such claims, *de jure*, if the problem of nation-making were simply to create a unit that should as nearly as possible resemble the greatest number of its own atoms.

They might have it, *de facto*, if numbers always expressed strength.

POLITICAL LIBERTY.

Political Liberty is freedom to live according to self-made Law. There can be no absolute Liberty except to an Ideal Nation—*i.e.* a Nation of ideal Human Beings. Liberty is the freedom to be absolutely spontaneous when spontaneity is infallibly good—*i.e.* the spontaneity of an ideal man—other freedom from all restrictions is not Liberty. Liberty, therefore, to an imperfect nation is to be found under the Law. Government should prevent one (individual) from interfering with the other's right practice.

THREE KINDS OF SOCIAL UNITY.

The dominant individual associating to itself inferior individuals as accessories of its comprehending individuality is Feudalism.

The many, either equal or of an inequality not arising to obvious supremacy in any one section of the community point to Nationalism.

Nationalism culminating in a chosen chief who

strikes the force downwards in a subtler feudalism— the action of the two systems coinciding tends to Constitutionalism.

Despotism. To those for whom Morality is fixed— a system of mental and bodily actions, having relation to external circumstances, and obligatory both in quantity and quality on all men, there can be no reasonable social organism but Despotism, civil and ecclesiastical.

Monarchy. There is this great advantage (among many others) in a Monarchy that it creates a *gradus* of rank (and consequently of social ambitions) irrespective of *direct political power*.

Now that the Parliament of England is no longer Christian—and rightly for the nation is not so—there is new need for an ultimate authority, wholly Christian, in which should reside the best sources of public opinion: a sun to radiate that general body politic whose *action* is through the heterogeneous parliament.[1]

[1] Mr. Dobell evidently here alludes to that scheme for 'a new round-table of Christian fellowship and activity,' which is so often spoken of in his earlier letters, and which, as is well known to his intimate friends, always occupied a large place in his thoughts: as it has done in the thoughts of other modern Philosophers—noticeable among whom is Dr. Arnold.—ED.

MEMORANDA ON THE THEORY OF OUR TERRESTRIAL LIFE.

That man or society who has every part of 'apostolic' character but the miraculous powers that alone can make that character permanent in this world among lower natures, is surely not the fittest to secure the progress of good.

All permanent political or social institutions must have a basis in the common qualities of mankind; so that no national retrogression and no degradation of the individual should ever be able to get below that basis; as in the case of an ethical creed for the individual—a set of moral motives—which must be such that his worst phases cannot get below its control. A Peerage that should be purely an *aristocracy* cannot be permanent; but a peerage built on wealth and acres—physical power—is safe in the worst times.

May it not be shown that all great Reforms arise not out of the good but bad qualities of the Reformers,—God so working by the foolishness of men? See the Religious Reformation grounded on the riches and wealth and power of the monastic clergy, though those things were the great barrier against the barbarism of aristocratic power, and were the means of enlightenment as compared with the lower clergy whom the Reformers praised. So in political reform and Bacon's inroad on Scholasticism.

MEMORANDA CONCERNING SPAIN.

A Nation should be one great Human Being, composed of many individual human beings in such organic relations as, without destroying numbers, render multiplicity into Unity. This is organic Unity.

Examining the conditions of organic unity in a smaller and more elementary case—the individual man for instance—we find among the primary principles of its existence this—that its material has throughout certain qualities which, whether in the given instance those of homogeneity or not, agree with those observable in true homogeneity ; the French express part of them when they say *connexité* (as distinct from connection), we might still further express them by such a word as syntithemic, but as their common sign is that they are the products of one producing machine—*e.g.* nail is not flesh, hair is not nail, flesh is not bone, but nail, flesh, hair and bone are produced by one digestive system—they might perhaps be best indicated by *homopœic*.

Now the peculiarity of the tract of country called Spain is that its inhabitants not only fail to be *homopæic* but are to a greater extent than those of any other civilized land in Europe *heteropæic*. Catalonia is not Spanish but Spain. Not an organic part of the Spanish whole, but nails, hair, flesh, bones, brain, heart, total Spain. So of the other provinces.

Spanish Bigotry is not an intellectual or spiritual preference for Papacy, but for a system that costs so little work and uncertainty—Religion apart from morals. Who would resign the comforts of such freedom for a creed that tonsures the conscience and transfers the endless casuistry of the schools to the centre of personal life?

A Republic should never be so large that it can by sudden action be dangerous to the rest of the World, nor so small as not to be powerful if persistent.

I think the medieval and post-medieval peoples desired *privilege* rather than liberty: the Republics being merely cities of nobles in relation to the rest of mankind and desiring and comprehending nothing other. When, then, and in what germinal form did the first feeling for liberty arise in Modern Europe?

It is curious to note that the great feudal Bishoprics to which Papacy owed so much of that power by which it controlled sovereigns were erected originally by sovereigns as a means of subjugating the people. See Montesquieu's 'Esprit des Lois.'

MEMORANDA CONCERNING THE HISTORY OF FLORENCE.

It should be borne in mind—that the tendency to over-individualism is the danger of small Republics: that this danger had been special in Florence from the special selfishness and turbulence of its citizens: that a great statesman might fairly theorize on these two memoranda with Medicean results; for an unrecognized Prince, unifying and subordinating by Monarchy without destroying the machinery of individualism would seem, in the given cases, to be the *sine qua non* of political welfare. Larger causes than Lorenzo had brought the Tuscan people to the state described by Villari (page 416) and Lorenzo is to be judged only in relation to such a moral condition of things. Granted the desideratum to maintain monarchy, without the forms of it, in Florence, and remembering the selfishness and turbulence of its past history, a statesman might require to regulate family alliances in the manner indicated.

PROPERTY AND COMMUNISM.

The question between Communism and Property is one of Education. Communism inverts the order of progress and demands the final result of Education. Communism says the communistic exercise of labour for all will develop love and delight. But in the imperfect what is to be the motive, before Love and Delight exist? Some compulsion. All compulsion acts on egotism.

Therefore you cultivate egotism as to Property, without the counteraction of the delight of giving.

Ephesians iv. 28—'let him labour'—'*that he may have to give.*'

2 Thessalonians iii. 8. 'Any man's bread.'

2 Thessalonians iii. 12. 'That with quietness they work and eat their *own bread.*'

1 Timothy iii. 4. 'his own house.'

1 Timothy iii. 12. 'their own houses.'

ARE 'FIELD-SPORTS' A BENEFIT TO SOCIETY?

Before answering this question consider that in every civilized community there must be a vast class of men wealthy enough to choose their own occupations and young enough or stupid enough to choose only those which please them. Then take some turns on the Pincian Hill, or on the Corso, or in any Spanish Alameda of a non-mountainous district, or on the Chiaja of Naples, or even the Allées or Place of those towns in France where Monsieur has no more fatiguing *chasse* than that of little birds. I don't think that even the cross between Sodom and Sacerdos, which you may see by the score in the Priests' Colleges at walk in the same places, is so hopeless a perversion of Manliness as you may observe (again by the score) in the faces (for instance) of young nobles in whom the fine facial lines, inherited from some medieval king-maker, have been emasculated by generations of effeminacy into the record, the expression, and the prophecy of every meaner vice. Then go to any great 'meet' of wealthy Englishmen and note the wholesome hearty courageous human nature, which, whatever their faults, distinguishes the face, make, and bearing of four of such men out of five.

Cruelty is measured not by the amount of pain inflicted but by the number of good qualities violated, and bad qualities encouraged, in a man by being the agent of that infliction.

JOURNALISM.

Literature involuntarily divides itself into two kinds; the one written to be sold, the other written irrespective of sale. In the polar extremes of each kind we shall find the specific difference in its highest exaggeration: and in the equatorial border-land at its zero. The right specimen of each being, of course, to be found where the specific are in just proportion to the generic qualities.

The kind for sale must, to sell, be in sufficient harmony with the buyers to be agreeable, and (to sell persistently), in such harmony with their conscience and intelligence as to be *permanently* agreeable. But continually to produce such requires higher intellectual powers than requisite to read it and, on the average, such intellectual powers imply a general mental congruity in their possessor and therefore a total superiority.

The tendency of literature produced by superiors, even though for the *agrément* of inferiors, is to represent, intentionally or involuntarily, that superiority. The natural condition, therefore, of a literature written for sale is such a mental superiority to the buyers as shall be consistent with complete *rapport. I.E.* that the agreement must always be greater than the difference. This kind, whether in books or newspapers, is Journalism, and we see that it exactly fulfils one of the great conditions of education. What at first sight seemed alarming and monstrous—that the instruction of the masses should be done by teachers and primers chosen by themselves, proves, therefore, to be one of the most necessary and beneficial processes of Nature,

QUÆSITUM.

Something which shall stand to written Fine-Art in the relation of the R.A. Exhibition to painted Fine-Art. Something so far supported by the qualified few as to make it representative of that fine minority, and so crowned by the highest social sanction as to attract the loyal observation of the People.

To the education of taste, national or individual, two processes, at least, are necessary—nourishment, by exercise and assimilation, and development by exercise and stimulus. Our present literary system, which regulates supply entirely by demand, provides for only one of these processes.

The elevating stimulus to the taste of the less qualified *many* should proceed from the taste of the more qualified few. Though the taste of those 'few' cannot personally act upon those 'many' it may do so through the representative action of those works of taste which it enjoys.

Those works, always a little in advance of popular taste, will themselves advance as the taste of the few advances, and, slowly proceeding towards the great standards of literary excellence, should be followed by the national progress. While we publish only what is certain to be profitable to the Publisher—*i.e.* what is certain to be largely popular—the taste of the few can have no such representative in current Literature. There is this difference between a rare picture and a poem: if there be one person in the world with sufficient cash and taste to appreciate it the picture sells, and the sale of it therefore does not necessarily prove a *public* up to its level: but a poem can only be published in a book, a book can only be published by editions, and editions cannot sell unless a corresponding troop of readers exist to buy i

MEMORANDA AND FRAGMENTS

OF

PROJECTED PLAY

MEMORANDA AND FRAGMENTS OF PROJECTED PLAY, 'THE COUNCIL OF ——.'

Introductory Note.—Among Mr. Dobell's papers have been found a number of scattered memoranda and fragments of the Drama originally intended to form a prominent portion of the second part of *Balder*. It was to have been performed before, or read to, Balder and his friends, whose comments would have been introduced. As the idea of the Play developed, and the materials for its working out accumulated, this intention was abandoned, and had '*The Council of* ——' ever been completed it would have been published as a separate book. But it may be well to remember that the purpose of the author was, by means of this play, to represent another side of that 'progress from Doubt to Faith, from Chaos to Order,' one phase of which was shown in Balder, Part the First. There is a memorandum of what is evidently designed to follow the conclusion of the Drama, where

Balder points out that 'it illustrates the contest between the two poles,—the One and the Many : the only reconciliation of which is when the One is that One of whom the Many is but the sub-division.' . . . Then, he is asked—'How came you by this Christianity ?—By vision, by Ecstasy?' Balder answers,—'Much more calmly and surely. I was in the very dust, I had found—I will say how another time—the impotence of Philosophy. I had trusted to the heart and found myself in the act of Murder. I found my whole soul crying out for a revelation of Truth, and I began to think that what was a necessity of Nature must exist somewhere. The thirsty eye sees water. The starving man beholds visible bread, by the instinct of the body for its want.'

It is thought that there exists much that is of interest and value, not only in the more finished passages of this Play, but among some of the merely fragmentary materials, appreciation of which may be assisted by outlines (collected and condensed from the memoranda) of the scheme, principal characters, and scenes.

The main idea of the Play is the struggle between the Church of Rome and the Secular Power, in the middle ages. This is represented by an imaginary episode of the long war between Guelf and Ghibelline. The time is about 1440. The scene, a plain in the South of Europe on which stands a city, with a hill-country, having Northern geology and temperature, at the back of the city. In this high hill-country stands the almost impregnable castle and village of a Heretic Knight. The whole country forms part of a Duchy which has been surrendered to the suzerainty of the Popes; but the last Duke, a profligate, has broken the fief, and his daughter, the present Duchess, has not yet renewed it.

The Archbishop, brother of the Pope and an aged devotee, has retired to a Monastery near the city. At the instance of his ambitious Chaplain, who hopes to rise in the overthrow of existing magnates, he has required the Pope to send a Cardinal to hold a Council, reform the Court,—where a Chancellor-Bishop reigns supreme,— and purge the city and its schools of heresy. The Cardinal comes with papal orders to this effect, but specially enjoined, (in consequence of the present jealousy of the Emperors in regard to papal fiefs) to obtain the voluntary re-surrender of the Duchy, if possible, and armed with a Bull to make him Sovereign-Nuncio in case of refusal.

The action of the play was designed to illustrate— 1st. the mistake of the Church of Rome in creating a machinery more powerful for evil in the hands of bad, than for good in the hands of good, men. This was to be shown by the contest between the Cardinal and the Chancellor and the eventual triumph of the Chancellor. 2nd.—The Mistake of the Church of Rome in creating a hierarchy of 'infallible' superiors to legislate for, and govern, general mankind. This was to be shown by the conflict between the Cardinal and the Philosopher,[1] a Teacher of great influence and authority in the City, whereby would be brought out the inconsistency of such hierarchies with the true order of human growth and progress, which requires *self*-government in view of ideal principles.

The Cardinal shows the best Roman Catholic theory, seen from the Catholic stand-point. The Chancellor shows the inherent vices of that theory. The Philosopher illustrates the essential warfare between Romanism and Knowledge; as Heretica shows the warfare between it and Truth. Other characters show various anti-papal principles, including the involuntary antagonisms of Science.

The Cardinal is noble and chivalrous; gentle and humble: losing himself in the being of the Church.

---

[1] No names had been decided on for any of the characters in the play. Throughout the Memoranda they are designated in this way. 'Forza' and 'Heretica' would seem only temporary substitutes for names ultimately to be chosen.

But, as he is the Church, the Church on great occasions becomes *him*, and he speaks with her individuality.

The Chancellor is wily, subtle, cynical, absolutely unscrupulous;—the type of clever, base, successful worldliness.

The old Archbishop, a fierce imbecile, the victim of his young and able Chaplain, is an illustration of the devotee Monk; his morbid veneration giving rise to endless and agonizing casuistries. The significant feature of his character is Worship of Authority.

His Chaplain represents Ambition fighting its way from the ranks; glorying in the Church as the *via sacra* for peasant to throne.

The Heretic Knight appears to be the embodiment of the brave, wise, kindly soldier.

Heretica, the *gouvernante* of the Knight's daughter, speaks for pure Christianity—the Religion of Love.

The Philosopher represents that indomitable spirit of struggle and search for Truth, on which the higher progress of the world depends, and he is therefore equally antagonistic to the noble and spiritually-minded Cardinal and to the corrupt and scheming Chancellor.

The first scene passes at the frontier of the Duch . An escort of soldiers has been sent to meet the Cardinal, and while awaiting his arrival talk among themselves of the Council, &c.

The Cardinal and his young Secretary enter.—Softened by memories, the Cardinal speaks in tender confidence—thus indicating his paternal affection for his devoted companion—of his own early youth and his lost love. He tells the story of his loss. He, the student son of a vassal, had raised himself to scholastic honours: she, the only daughter of Count —— who had sided with the serfs in a peasant war. War breaking out, the student left his College to lead the peasants. They were defeated. Her father's castle was stormed by the army of the enraged nobles. The Lover, wounded, lying helpless within sight of the castle, saw Father, Mother, Daughter, brought forth for instant execution. A faithful follower stole him, senseless, from the field and reported him slain. He, recovering strength, sought a distant country, concealed his name, now under the ban of attainder, and entered the Church. He has not re-entered that country till now, when he comes as a Prince over its nobles.

When alone, the Cardinal, in apostrophe to his early love shows how she is and has been, though 'dead,' an abiding presence with him, and beseeches her whose exquisite womanhood has been so long his proxy with the virgin Perfection, to interpose for him constantly during the great Task to which he is going.

> 'I shone on her and, chaster than the moon,
> She gave me back my light.'

Scene in Palace reception room. Nobles talking of the Cardinal and his Mission, the precise object of which is yet unknown. Chancellor talking with Nobles subtly suggests objects personal to each interlocutor as menaced by the Mission. Cardinal enters and is formally welcomed by Duchess, Chancellor and Nobles. He declines the cold offer of the Duchess to sit by her, saying that he must learn to know his colleagues—and walks round the crowded room, pausing by each knot of talkers and joining the argument. Passing by the Duchess he is heard to say—

> 'Quale manus addunt ebori decus,
> Little th' old Roman wot whereof he spake.'—

She is pleased and sends fresh invitation to him; he sits in her circle and converses of feasting, dress, beauty, &c.

Various remarks from knots of observers round the room.

Chancellor (?) ' —— My Lord of ——
Riding his Pegasus, the churchly palfrey
Of my poor wit capered to see him prance
As thus—nay, my good lord, as the fair jewel
Upon her royal breast, were there a touch
So blest as might essay it, would be found
To have drawn a vital joy from the warm white
It lies on, seems it not unto your eye
That yon poor toy doth milk a human light
From the rich hand that holds it?'

Scene in Castle of Heretic Knight. It is his daughter's wedding day and he is surrounded by friends and guests in the banqueting hall. Entrance of Heretica, who tells him the Bride awaits his blessing and last words. He suggests to each friend some amusement to his taste—and shows to the philosopher a new improvement in the Block-book which lies on the table, an invention of one of the friends. Philosopher and Heretica are left alone, and converse on the subject of the Cardinal's mission. Philosopher tells her that the Cardinal is to attend his next lecture in person. Shall he give one that is negatively untrue to his real beliefs, or one that embodies them? He sets forth the whole question of tests, &c., and asks Heretica's feeling. She urges *truth*, without ostentation or reserve. He promises it. Then they speak of the Papacy and the intrinsic antagonism between it and knowledge. He speaks of his own outgrowing of the monastic forms; and instances the various modes in which the mind of the devotee receives the name of God, whether syllabling it, in silence, or shutting all the eyes of the soul to *feel* it pass as a spirit;—of the festering of the galled brain; of yearnings towards a new devotion. They turn to Plato, to explain her difficulty in a passage. Thence he brings in theory of Ideals and the Democratic inferences therefrom. Thence—illustrating the varieties of human mind in its gradations towards the ideal—to a system of Divine Physiology. Thence to the consequent sacredness of science, and—as consequent on this Divine nature of the Universe, its progressive character, which is inconsistent with the stereotyped system of a Papal Church. Heretica opposes to his metaphysics her own simple faith. She is content to know the Beginning and the End,—God and the sensible world. That is sufficient for her. She seeks not to find out. Among the wonderful and glorious non-intelligible, there is a wonderful and glorious intelligible—Man. She is sure that God will speak to her through that which *can* speak.

Asked what is God she answers 'Love.' Certain of the principle she is at rest as to its application. The Philosopher tries to show the essential agreement of his philosophy—*e.g.* that the Universe in its beauty *is* Love visible; not a creature, but an action; the Λόγος is Mankind.

Scene between Chancellor and Baron Forza, one of the most powerful nobles about the Court. The Chancellor tells Forza that the chief object of the Cardinal's Mission is against *them*; that whoever escapes, they are both too conspicuous for pardon. He gives evidence of this which convinces the Baron, who asks what must be done in defence, as time presses. The Chancellor answers, for the present, nothing,—but find opportunity for action. They two, wit and strength, must provide the element most favourable to them—chaos and commotion. 'The powers of the world are Nature's; we use them and guide them. If the present order remains we are unnecessary, but bring Chaos, and society cannot do without us. The Cardinal, before the day of the Council which is to try *us*, has appointed a day for the trial of sundry small offenders. We must provide him with such as shall turn the world upside down. Will any dare touch us till we have set it on its legs again? And before then,—what not?'

For the present, therefore, his object is to postpone the meeting of the Council. Now, there is a band of heretics among the hills so strong in numbers and in popularity that the Church has not yet touched them, nor the Knight, their beloved Chief. The Baron must cause this Chief to be taken prisoner, 'by command of the Cardinal;' seizing him in the midst of his retainers, whose revenge will probably be fatal to the Cardinal. Forza reminds the Chancellor of the Heretic Knight's friend, the Philosopher, who is adored by the wild students of the City, and asks if he, too, shall be taken? The Chancellor replies that nothing must be done against him yet, as he is in league with a faction of Republican artizans whom certain Florentines have infected.

Baron.—'So much the better! They will be raised against the Cardinal, and can afterwards be crushed.'

Chancellor.—'No; the peasantry of the country are too much in the power of their Lords to be useful to the Church, but it is to the *canaille* of towns that the Church must look for her future support. It is by creating a new set of burgher-dignitaries, chosen by this civic mob (a mob of freemen, not serfs) and gradually encouraging this new order till it supplants that of the nobles, that the Church can extend and keep her power. This *canaille* must always be in the hands of the Priests and its voice, therefore, however apparently free, will be the voice of the Church. But these boors can make no distinction. Their whole being, beyond the born brute, is a kind of canine *habit*. Therefore, if they once bark at the Priesthood, our rule is over. Cardinal or Chancellor is but Priest in their eyes, and to attack one is to break loose from all. We must therefore use them, but not in this way. How I see not yet, but shall see.'

Meanwhile, there must be some certain way of knowing, in advance, the movements of the enemy. The complicity of the new Chaplain must be secured. Forza exclaims that it is he who has been the very means of bringing about the Cardinal's Mission. The Chancellor replies, he will be the less suspected.

The chivalrous Cardinal sends his Chaplain to the Chancellor, with the items of accusation against him. The Chancellor thus obtains the desired opportunity of suborning the Chaplain,—who, putting all the various temptations together on one side, and the chance of the Cardinal's failure on the other, concludes that a game may be played with both sides, by which in either event he must win. Meditates to himself, after the interview, somewhat thus :—'The wise man says, be prepared for any fate. I say, be prepared for thy friend's fate also: for how saith the Scripture,—" Do unto others," &c., if " as they should do unto you," then surely as you would do to yourself. *Ergo*, as I prepare for my own fate, I prepare for my Master's. And surely it were ingratitude to so good a Master to suffer his misfortunes to do me harm.'

Battle scene.

FRAGMENT OF CAVALRY SONG.

The merry sun shines, the merry birds sing,
   The merry leaves dance as we go;
Blow, trumpets, blow, to the clump, clamp, cling,
   Blow, jolly trumpets, blow!

Heretic Knight addresses his men.—'I am an old man; who knows but in thrashing this hare-brain bounds-breaker I may over-do myself and need to sleep? Take my will to my son. If we are beaten you need say nothing, the lands will go to Mother Church, and you know what a landlady she is, by many a near example. But tell him, if we conquer,—as, with God's help I doubt not we shall,—that I hold every widow and orphan made among us this day as children of the house.

He shall be next of kin to every one of them. This is my last testament made before all men. Now then ;—for Victory.' He goes on to speak scornfully of the enemy. 'This Monster that moves up against us,—has it a mouth like Hell? does it puff with the bellows of tempests? will it drown us in the red rivers of its veins? The heart on't is no bigger than a man's' . . . . Just before the engagement, the Knight goes down his line of adherents, speaking a word to each, calling to mind some old deed of valour, some benefit given or received, some trait of family story &c., &c.

[In the engagement that follows, Baron Forza is killed—and the remainder of the Chancellor's schemes connected with him fall to the ground.]

The Duchess, who has fallen in love with the Cardinal, visits him, and, in royally equivocal language acquaints him with her fancy. He takes the innocent side of the *équivoque*, and she, puzzled, leaves him with invitation to sup with her and to confess her. During 'Confession' Scene, he shows this wrathful, despotic Juno, who professes to despise Duty, Obedience, and Virtue, that her professions are false—that it is a Jove to master and humble her whom she really needs. She admits this; and entreats him to be that Jove. He answers her so nobly—at first with lofty indignation, and afterwards, in tender and compassionate exhortation—leading her by questions, through the memories of Child, Maiden, early love—that he awes her, and then subdues her to a love that takes the form of penitence. [This, however, is but a transient state of mind with her, and, later on, her vanity and evil passions are so artfully played on, directly and indirectly, by the Chancellor, as to turn her so-called love to a bitter and revengeful hatred, which is made one of the many means whereby he secretly attacks the Cardinal.]

The Trial Scene. When the Heretic Knight is brought before him, the Cardinal treats him with the honour and consideration due to his years and bearing, and to give him time to collect his thoughts for the conflict of wits that must ensue, calls on the next case. —Heretica enters, accompanied by her pupil, the Knight's daughter, to whom she is talking with lofty cheerfulness and courage. During the preliminaries of her trial the Cardinal is quite silent. When she is called on to address the Court, she begins to speak collectedly, till after steadfastly regarding the Cardinal, she suddenly breaks off—shrieks and turns away with a passionate prayer to God to spare her from one last, worst agony.

'Thus madly crying out, she sinks insensible. The Cardinal is silent, and remains silent while they bear her away. After an interval, he gives orders that she shall be brought in again, before the rising of the Court, and commands that meanwhile the other cases shall proceed. In judging them, he displays exquisite and unnecessary ingenuity and hair-splitting subtlety of intellect, keen and pitiless hardness,—alternating with curious mistakes and momentary misapprehensions. When this change is apparent in the Cardinal, the Chancellor instantly causes the Philosopher and others who have escaped lightly earlier in the day, to be re-arraigned, and so condemned. The Prosecutor then, in a speech, accuses the Heretic Knight, who requests to be assigned learned assistance. The Cardinal assigns him his Chaplain, who makes a defence of voluble casuistry. The Knight, interrupting, addresses the Cardinal, disclaiming all such subtleties; and himself replies to the accusation in a simple, noble speech, conveying his own plain theory of Religion as distinct from Philosophy, and giving Scripture for his authority. He denies the Church as the medium of the Holy Spirit; illustrating his view of the case by describing the sand made vitreous, transparent and prismatic by fire, by which change the opaque sand transmits and reflects the light which was always round it, but wherewith its own nature was incompatible; pointing out that the sand has risen in the order of things, and but for having so risen, the light could not have been within it and through it. Yet sand and glass are not the light. Further he says that 'the day may come when every Man shall be a priest, and the Monarchs of the world shall be judged by the Universal Church of Mankind.'

The Cardinal, in giving judgment, first demolishes the Chaplain's defence by exposing its logical errors, then with cold loftiness he answers the Knight, denouncing the pursuit of *Truth* and stating the inevitably evil future results thereof. Condemns him.

Heretica is then brought in again. During the pause of expectation before her re-appearance, one of the spectators asking another who she is, is answered that men whisper her to be the daughter of the good Count—the well-remembered protector of the serfs. That she was supposed to be killed, with her father and mother, when their castle was taken and destroyed, but that though carried thence, apparently dead, to the grave shown to this day, as hers—she had been restored to life, and had ever since been sheltered and protected in the family of the Heretic Knight to whose daughter she became *gouvernante* and friend.

Heretica is very calm and self-possessed. She

speaks; calling on the Cardinal to do what he knows to be his duty, and showing how the warfare between them must be to the death. He answers. They each address the other in words enigmatical to the audience but comprehensible to themselves, and conveying the certainty of doom. Then he condemns her.

Fresh spectators enter, and question—'Which is the Cardinal?' They are told. 'What! Yonder grey-haired man?' 'Grey-haired!' The fact is evident, and gradually it circulates through the Court, and murmurs of astonishment are heard. The Cardinal inquires the reason of these murmurs and presently learns wherefore all eyes are fixed on him in such amazement. He rises with calm dignity and tells the wonderers that since this great thing has happened even in their sight, they should praise God for thus vouchsafing to him who —young as to earthly years—comes as a Judge among them, this sudden and visible crown of reverence and authority.

The populace recognize the Miracle, and the Court rises.

After the Trial Scene, a brief interview takes place between the Chaplain and Secretary, in which the former says that Heretica has established her claim to the character of Sorceress which popular report gives her, since she evidently possesses the power of turning men's hearts at her will, and has most certainly exercised this power upon the Cardinal.

The Secretary, believing this and alarmed for his master, is summoned to that master's presence.—The Cardinal after many terrible hours of meditation has resolved to make one supreme effort to save Heretica from the destruction both bodily and spiritual which he believes to be imminent. He will see her; he will visit her in her prison; not as Prince and Judge, but disguised in the dress of his youth, that he may appeal to her with sacred memories of the look, the voice, the touch of other times, and thus have power to change and save her. He therefore bids the Secretary procure such a disguise, and further charges him to go to the Governor of the Castle, and, showing the official seal, give notice that an old friend of Heretica's is to be admitted to her cell, under authority of the Cardinal.

The Secretary goes to the Governor, but beseeches him to refuse admission, notwithstanding the Cardinal's order, to the mask who will that night come to see Heretica,—on the ground of her well-known sorceries, and his (the Secretary's) solicitude for the welfare of the masked visitor. The Governor carelessly declines to interfere, and the other entreats with no effect, till at last, growing desperate, he lets fall the fact that it is a life of the utmost value which is about to be exposed to these dangerous arts. The Governor still expresses himself content with the Cardinal's authority, as sufficient to save him from all consequences. The Secretary, in final desperation, confesses that the intending visitor to Heretica is the Cardinal himself. The Governor is aroused, and perceives the situation. Like all the other existing magnates of the Duchy, he is an enemy to the Cardinal and his mission of reform, and he now bids the Secretary wait while he considers,—and straightway goes to the Chancellor, who is at that moment in consultation with the Chaplain in another part of the Castle. The strange intelligence brought by the Governor is hailed by them as a certain assistance to their machinations against the Cardinal. The Chancellor orders that the Secretary shall be blindfolded and brought before him, and he himself questions him. The Secretary, almost frantic with anxiety and fear, is an easy prey to this astute and wily questioner, who soon draws from him all he needs to know. Affecting disbelief, he asks what motive can be assigned for the Cardinal's visit to Heretica? The Secretary answers,—he loves her. But this is scouted as being beyond all reason. How can he love her whom he never saw till she was placed before him on her trial? The Secretary declares that she is an Enchantress, and has assumed the form of the good Count ——'s daughter, the Cardinal's early love, in order to bewitch and to destroy him. The Chancellor is not to be beguiled by such tales, and threatens his victim with flagellation—then and there. The Secretary, in a passion of wild terror, and as a last resource, shows the Seal. The Chancellor takes it for a moment, and with it affixes seal to a blank parchment. Then restoring it, he orders the Secretary to be released, having established his authority, and promising to grant what he requires. The blind-folded Secretary is taken away, therefore, still trembling, but happy; and the Chancellor and Chaplain congratulate one another. Directions are given that the mask is to be admitted to Heretica's cell. This love-passage will appeal to the Archbishop's ruling idea, and he must be got to sign a letter to the Pope demanding the degradation of the Cardinal. Upon the parchment with the Ducal Seal, another letter to the Pope must be written, threatening to make over the Duchy to the Anti-pope unless the Chancellor is appointed Nuncio in place of the Cardinal. Within an hour must be provided the swiftest horse and strongest man to ride for life or death with these letters, and bring the answers back. The

Chaplain asks who shall be chosen for this momentous charge, and how best can they arrange for the needful speed and security. The Chancellor rebukes him for his folly in wasting thought on matters whereon others can be made to think. The true wisdom of affairs is to apply the motive power to machinery already made by Nature. The Heretic Knight's son-in-law is, with his Bride, under sentence to be burned. First pardon him, lest his selfishness get the better when the chance of escape occurs, and then promise that if he can bring back the answering letters from the Pope by a certain hour, his Bride shall also be pardoned and set free. Nature will do miracles of wit and labour, pricked by such spurs.

'Cheer up my Chaplain—Bishop—what you will.
Now, for a wink, the world's ungovernëd,
And I'll be Jove on't. . . .

'. . . . His (*the Cardinal's*) good saint nods ;
There is a gap in Fortune, and our wills
Must fill it ere he wakes.'

When the Cardinal returns from the interview with Heretica, the Secretary—hoping to hear that no such interview has taken place—eagerly asks if it has been successful. The Cardinal answers mystically by a reference to a passage from St. Augustine in which St. Augustine speaks of the soul of St. Jerome as having appeared to him with 'grat lite and sweet savours and words of swech comfort as St. Augustine would never write,' but says he shall see her once again—who can tell what Grace in the meantime may have done with his words?

[That this second interview did not take place we learn from a memorandum which states that the Cardinal, on his way to open the Council, meets the crowd *returning from the burning of Heretica*, which, *at her own request*, has taken place a day before the appointed time. The reason of this, doubtless, Heretica's desire to spare the Cardinal any further mental conflict.

The Cardinal, to gain breathing time, halts at the shrine of the Madonna of ———.]

Last Scenes.—The Council, on the day of the Chancellor's trial. Notwithstanding all efforts at further postponement, the day and hour have arrived, before any sign of the approach of the Envoy returning with letters from the Pope. In the outer chamber there is a throng of soldiers, guards and people—eager to hear what goes on within the great Hall of the Council. Messengers come in and pass out again, dropping items of news,—how the Cardinal's speech of accusation proceeds,—how it is received. From the movement, excitement, confusion, and clash of voices of all this, the scene changes to the grand Hall, where in solemn state and magnificence the Council sits. The Cardinal having, at the beginning, stated that the disasters of the Duchy have chiefly arisen from the incapacitating illness of the Archbishop, has caused an empty chair, representing the absent Ecclesiastical Ruler, to be placed beside that of the Duchess, while he himself takes his place in one of the side semicircles. Then, in a speech designed to rouse the Council and stimulate it to its highest sense of justice, he states the heads of the various charges against the Chancellor which are to be proved by the evidence that is to follow. Finally, he tells them that 'of great misfortunes there are two kinds,—one, where the heart knoweth its own bitterness, and the stranger doth not intermeddle therewith : the other, where the personal injury is also felt in its rebound from the external world. Among states, these are ensampled, the first, by such evils as are compatible with respect abroad ; the second, by those which, like the sores of Lazarus, attract the flies and dogs of foreign injury and contempt. The wicked in high places are infallible causes thereof. Therefore, in coming to purge your state from this internal ill which is attracting so swarming an outer exasperation, I am acting, not as a foreign protector, but as a humble and patriotic citizen. I am certain of your hearty assistance in determining the Truth of the things which witnesses shall depose. But, first, I will call on the accused to say whether he be content to be judged by you.'

The Chancellor rises. [During his speech, Messengers keep coming to him with whispered tidings,—1st. that his Envoy is known, by signal, to be five miles off. 2nd. Crossing the ford, two miles off.   3rd. Carried away by the current.   4th. Escaped from the river lower down, and again riding towards the city. 5th. Riding up the road to the city gate.   6th. At the gate.   7th. In the street.   8th. At the great door of entrance to the Council Hall.] As he begins, 1st Messenger enters. He bursts into an eulogium on the irresistible power of oratory, and declares that though innocent of the things charged against him, he wishes to be condemned, and will then do all in his power by disclosing his knowledge of internal affairs, to assist in the purification of the state. The Cardinal, answering what he says of oratory, warns the Council that there are two kinds of orators, one, by whom it is well to be guided, who by his eloquence raises the minds of his audience to their highest and noblest phasis ; the other, against whom it is needful to be on guard, who by subtle appeal to lower interests and passions would move his judges against their conscience. The Chancellor resumes : He is sure that they, his judges, who have so intimately shared in his past life, who have so constantly acted with him in his official career, are convinced against him. It is a terrible and curious fact that sentence on an accused is not passed by the witnesses against him, nor by his crimes, but by the judges who are bound by no necessity to judge according to the evidence. He has no hope, therefore. Nay, such is the power of oratory, he has no care. Though innocent of everything laid to his charge, his soul is convinced of sin. He is weary of life and of himself. True, he is guiltless of the crimes attributed to him, but there are other evil doings heavy on his soul. He will make no defence. Condemn him. The sentence will be unjust, *quoad* the accusations, but he will engage to justify it ; for he swears, that before he leaves this tribunal for the cloister, he will disgorge his memory of every unrighteousness, small and great. [Here, there is some perceptible movement among certain Bishops and Barons of the Council.] He is happy in that some of his judges know so intimately the affairs of the state, and how far corruption exists. If, in their judgment, his fall can assist in the needful purgation, he will rejoice to be the sacrifice ; nay, nothing that his knowledge and experience can reveal shall be wanting to assist so holy a work. Moreover, he could rejoice in his own fall, from a higher than any temporal consideration. It is held by some, to whose learning and ability he humbly defers—that a time shall come in which the Church will dominate the whole world, and temporal princes be reduced to the mere sceptres in the hand of ecclesiastical power. If, by this forcible assumption of sovereign rights and the transfer of himself from the steps of his sovereign's throne to the footstool of the Papal Legate, he can be made a precedent whose glorious successions shall be a *scala sancta* to that Heaven to which good churchmen aspire, he will be ready to bless the sacrificial hand. . . . There is another possible benefit to the community of which he may be the unworthy instrument. It is held by some that the cities are rising into dangerous prosperity and power,—that an unordained and popular aristocracy is growing more and more formidable. He confesses to have assisted towards this—by measures he has introduced or countenanced. In his fall, the opposite party will perhaps gain a victory that may compensate for the evil to which he has been the unintentional accessory.

Thus, the Chancellor appeals alternately to each class represented by the different Members of the Council. Finally, he dilates on the rapture which he, as a churchman, will feel in the elevation of the Church paramount. But there is one inevitable condition,—it must be with the assent of all other classes. If, by their vote to-day, they show their submission, how happy is he to be the occasion thereof!

The Duchess, perceiving the effect on the Council of his speech, here interrupts with praise of the Chancellor for his humility, and saying that, as yet, he is innocent in the eyes of his judges, she calls him to the chair of honour at her side. He deprecates; but several voices call on him to go up. Turning to the Council, he humbly beseeches them not to let personal feelings interfere with their conviction as to his deserts; not to remember (enumerating them) his services to the state. With these great charges hanging over him he cannot ascend to that seat. He knows the pain it must be to them to formularize a painful verdict. He will give them no such pain. Let him but remain in the *place* of the accused, and he will accept it as a silent decision against him.

There are cries on all sides that he shall go up. After more deprecation and feigned reluctance, [during this 2nd Messenger enters,] he mounts the steps.

The Cardinal commands him to descend. He remains. The Cardinal calls on one after the other of those nobles on whom he had specially relied, to aid him in the exercise of his rightful authority. One after the other excuses himself.

The Cardinal then causes the Bill to be read by which he is appointed Sovereign-Nuncio, and himself ascends to the vacant chair, calling on the Duchess to order the removal of the Chancellor. On refusal, he threatens instant excommunication. The Chancellor whispers to the Duchess that all depends on gaining time—even one half hour. The Duchess demands that if she is to be excommunicated it shall be in due form. The Cardinal orders that the bells of interdict shall be sounded, and proceeds to the ceremonies preparatory to her excommunication. At the commencement of these ceremonies the 3rd Messenger enters, announcing that the Envoy has been carried away by the current. The Chancellor tells the Chaplain that all is lost unless the mob of students, &c., is let in before the excommunication is completed.

The ceremonies continue; during which, in rapid succession, enter the fourth and other messengers. On the arrival of the eighth bearing the Papal letters, the Chancellor shouts to the priests to hold—on peril of their souls!—and unfolds a heavy scroll before the Cardinal, with a torrent of invective ordering him to descend. A Herald proclaims the Chancellor sovereign-nuncio.

The Cardinal denounces the whole as a deceit of the adversary; shows that it is incredible, after being sent especially to degrade the Chancellor, that he, the Chancellor, should be thus exalted over him, and declares that only force shall remove him from that chair.

Guards, at the command of the Chancellor, rudely drag the Cardinal down, and disrobe him. Breaking from them, he turns to the Council and in solemn protest declares that nothing can take those thunders from his hands which he holds as the Vicegerent of God,—describes how invisible powers are following the beck of his naked finger . . . .

Duchess—to an attendant—'Here, fellow—take my shoe and strike the blasphemer on the mouth. I would I were a man to tread him in mine own person.'

The Chancellor, who is now invested with the robe of office, rises and tells the Cardinal he must learn that his boasted power will not so much as protect his lips from retribution. Then, in a few stately words, he addresses the Council, saying that the Cardinal had already told them it was a Court convened for great purposes, and that the event would justify it,—but otherwise than he supposed. The criminal is great indeed,—so great that an hour since he held in his hand all the forces of the Universe. Returning on the Cardinal, he passes rapidly over all the charges against him, culminating in that of Heresy,—Heresy in him who had caused Heretics to burn like frankincense,—Heresy, evidenced by sympathy and collusion with a known and condemned Heretic.

The Cardinal passionately demands who dares to testify these things of him? The Chancellor points to the young Secretary, who, stricken with remorse and despair, sinks at the Cardinal's feet.

Cardinal.—' *Thou*—?'

Secretary.—' Should I have left thee to Satan—to the Sorceress?'

Cardinal.—' *Thou*—?'

Secretary bursts into more desperate justification—but is still only answered by the one word—' *Thou*—?' He implores his master not to look on him . . . .

The mob of Students, &c. rush in—and a pike is aimed at the Cardinal's back. The Secretary starts from his knees and receives it in his breast,—the breast, uncovered by one of the crowd in order to staunch the blood flowing from the wound, is found to be a Woman's.

Outcry, amid which the mob from without increases in numbers and in fury—some crying 'Death to the Murderer of the Heretic Knight'—others,—' Death to the Murderer of the good Count ——'s daughter.' The Cardinal is struck down and killed.

The Chaplain suddenly enters with announcement of the death of the Archbishop.

Chancellor orders guards to clear the Hall—they disperse students, mob, &c. and remove the body of the Cardinal.

Then the Chancellor solemnly calls on the Council to proceed with its next business—the canonization of the departed saint—the Archbishop.

Sacred music sounds—and procession of priests enters.

MEMORANDA AND FRAGMENTS CONCERNING PRINCIPAL CHARACTERS.

THE CARDINAL.

[Memoranda concerning his character and the theories to be developed by him.]

> His right
> Points wrongly, like the mast of a stranded ship,
> Less Heavenward for sheer rectitude.

Let the Cardinal describe a true gentleman—*i.e.* one who in least things as in largest carries out the *principles* of Christ's character. Pointing out that the Graces are the Charities in Greek.

Let him describe the gradations by which he came to sum up all wishes in to be good and to see others good.

Let him show that the great thing in Life is not to do many things, but to do some things perfectly.

Let him describe true married Love after Paul's idea ('as Christ the Church').

Let him show *within what limits* only it is wise to interpose between men and the 'natural' results of their own imperfections.

Cardinal.—' Discipline your bodily functions to the truthful expression of your soul. Then *be* what you would seem and you will seem it.'

NUCLEI.

(*For the Cardinal, concerning 'our terrestrial Life.'*)

Whatever is to exist healthily on the earth must have its root therein and grow out thereof, even though its top should reach to Heaven.

All earthly institutions must have the physical Laws for Body wherein as Soul shall reside the higher Principles. The more highly, subtly, elaborately, they are exhibited and exercised in that Body the more freely, joyously, gloriously will that Soul be active in it.

Those Principles are the corolla and fragrance of those Laws, but no more to be expected in connection with the lower and cruder manifestations of them than the flower of the rose upon its root, or its perfume in the vesicles of the stem.

Let the Cardinal show the need for Self-denial.

While the human being is so far from the Ideal, and every lust is in ascendant by turns, we who set the example to mankind must do it by self-denial—the domination of theory—(ideal perceived by intellect) over spontaneity.

A happier time may come when the good man may live out an ideal life on earth, and may have as his highest duty the impersonation of that beautiful idea—a life in which every earthly good may be enjoyed as an ideal man would enjoy it, and therefore be made holy and beneficial, as contrasted with the same externalities when possessed by the evil, and therefore degraded to symbols of evil,—*e.g.* Beauty of tasteful environment as distinct from 'the pomps and vanities of this wicked world,' &c. &c. When the rich man is as if he were poor the precept against riches does not apply. When the fashion of mankind has changed the uses of wealth from carnal corruption to æsthetic and philanthropic benefactions the rich man may be nearest the 'kingdom of Heaven.'

Let the Cardinal set forth the pattern of a noble human life upon earth. A pyramid based *upon* earth. A congeries of *excellencies*: having no element *not* common to all men and no element *as* common to all men. A life such as every man *might* lead but no man *does* lead. In which the things done are *not* those which men do rarely, but the common acts of men done in a rare spirit. In which the goods of Life are not aliened from its own use for the use of others but distributed *per* its own use to the use of others—and therein glorified, as the tree exhales its saps in fruits and perfumes. Such a life by keeping within the hope appeals to the ambitions of all men, and being, like Man himself, a Divine within a corporeal, reconciles a present and a future world and the Word with the Work of God.

It agrees also with the arrangements of that Cosmos in which the subtler is secerned from the grosser not by separation but by union.

There are three modes of giving—the mechanical, the physiological, the Theocratic. The second is that for man, whose gifts should not be donation but communication—which is the mode of animated Nature.

Thou art a plant, thy neighbour is a bee. If he were just like thee he would have been treated like thee. Give him the dung that feeds thee, he starves. Digest and convert it into honey, he is happy and fat. And in the process thou hast also, out of what was to him valueless, assimilated wood, leaf, flower, to thine own beauty, the benefit of other neighbours, having yet other wants, and the glory of God in His World.

The Eucharist is an analogue of Life, which should be not to eat but to eat *with*. Eat thy bread and let thy neighbour starve—thy God is thy belly. Starve thyself by giving thy bread to thy neighbour—perchance being full he says 'who is the Lord?' *Com*municate—break thy bread *with* thy neighbour and by the thanksgiving and the sweet graces of that soul of thine which thy bread strengtheneth he, enjoying with thee, receives a charity more precious than bread.

Live therefore a life in which all thy good wants shall be exquisitely—not riotously—gratified, but so gratified that the gratification involves the welfare of others in the means and a *com*munication in the end.

When all the other wants are gratified there will remain one, of all most exquisite in its exercise—the want to give without even the semblance of return or advantage. This also gratify as the flower of life, but see that thy being is more than this flower, for a flower hath no power to endure upon the earth and without root and leaves perisheth swiftly, to the derision rather than to the good example of men.

The moralist should understand the *physiology* of virtue and what non-virtues are germs or cognates of virtue.

A full human character must have all these as the necessary *sine quibus non* of the others—the origins or nutritions or protections of them. A very complex *corpus* of such is requisite before the virtues proper come into place; and it is an ignorance of this that starves and deforms morals.

The Roman made his temple to Honour entered through the temple of Virtue—and he did well, for to him Honour was the ideal *Virtus*. We must (conversely) make our temple to Virtue entered by the Prophylæa of sacred Honour. These prophylæa are sacred because the profanation of them weakens the safety of the *sanctum sanctorum*.

Acting on the above let the Cardinal punish the layman who is brought before him for insulting the dirt of the Friars, and the Friars for being dirty. The one has violated the reverence which protects more important things, the other the cleanliness which is a safeguard of virtue.

THE CARDINAL ON FORBIDDING OF SCRIPTURES TO LAITY. PRO.

The Church does well to deny the Bible to the world, since the New Testament records the application of Christian Principles to a transition time of exceptional circumstances, while the duty of the Christian requires the application of them to noble and permanent life in the normal circumstances of the World.

This Book has to be made a human institution, a living flesh and blood. In such a transformation it is the same in essence, different to the eye.

You ask for the Book? I say behold it alive—translated into Men.

The Commonality are not competent to know the signs of such identity. Take Manna from Heaven, feed upon it till it is living humanity. I say it is the Manna, and more really the Manna than what is closer in phenomenal likeness.

But will your clown say so? And will you suffer him to compare the Manna with the flesh and blood?

RESULTS OF INTRODUCTION OF PRINTING.

Cardinal to Secretary: vision of the new world that must arise, of unforeseeable customs, opinions, feelings, if printing and other new powers raise the millions into thinking and *willing* Beings.

A forevision and prediction of the results of printing—especially in its future evocation of a race of unconsecrated *preachers*, a renewal of the old Athenian *Orators*—and demonstration of the vital necessity to extirpate it.

FOR CARDINAL'S SPEECH ON RECEIVING SUBMISSION OF TEMPORAL POWERS.

The ideal of the Race the ideal of an individual—soul and body—brain, permeating nerves and senses; hands, arms, bones, muscles, *et viscera*. Apply this to the offices and *ordo* of Church and state.

Let the Cardinal dilate (to his secretary) on the exquisite beauty of the Papal Church as the soul of this body the world, the sun of the social system, &c., &c., &c., showing the analogies with physical arrangements.

After this scene let Balder make comments to his friends showing the truth in this and the fault in the application. The round Table the Church to which it really applied.

CARDINAL'S THEORY CONCERNING CHURCH AND STATE.

The Empire (and all temporal power) the representation of the Natural Man: the Church the representation of the Holy Spirit.

If it be said that 'the powers that be are ordained (set in place) of God,' so are the various members of the human body, yet the Apostle shows the inferiority of some and the Saviour commands the cutting off of others—ay and casting into the fire.

That the Church did not immediately take her relative place, and is right in the slow movement to assume it, see even the chicken in the egg, where at first the *disjecta membra* are disordered, and afterwards the head is below the wing.

As the Individual Man is a federation of faculties so must be that great man—the Race. The Greeks acted on this Truth—as on all other Truths—*without knowing it*, in their many states, but they failed to feel that there must be a permanent head—that Athens or Sparta must not dominate by turns.

In justification of that last step of the Church by which Kings were equalized, *quoad* the Church, with common men the Cardinal must take the allegory of the body.

In the natural body of the natural man how awful and sacred a summit is the *head*—draw the subjection and reverence of the other parts to it. Yet when one comes to consider it the head is really the potential members, and the members are but the head descending into action. Consequently even the head when the natural man becomes converted is subject to that Holy Spirit which alights on it and dwells in it. We mark the forehead with the Cross and shave and anoint the crown.

Let the Cardinal show the possibility that the Universe is of Divine substance, and yet is not God, by the human mind in dreams, where every member of the dream Drama is a modification of your substance yet cannot be *addressed* as *you*, being often indeed in violent contrariety to you.

Found an argument for the Cardinal on puppets in a Hand. The Hand does all, but what is done is modified by the nature of the puppet. Ourselves, therefore, the proximate cause of what happens to us, though we do nothing; and though God be, as Creator of the puppet, the Primary Cause.

Let the Cardinal illustrate the archetypal world and its action on matter by the *immersion* of a Mould in water.

Let him show that Truths are usually accepted by Mankind for wrong reasons.

Let the Cardinal show the necessary connection of Papacy and *Monarchy*—and the same of political democracy with Religious Schism.

NUCLEI FOR CARDINAL.

Apart from all ecclesiastical considerations and arguments if a Church (an organized Priesthood) is the embodiment and extravasation of the *conscience* of Mankind there can be no doubt it should take, among those forms which embody the other mental qualities, that place which the thing it embodies takes among other things embodied.

Since excommunication of Kings produced deposition by virtue of its effect on the minds of *subjects*, the Papal permission of Heresy would have been suicidal. And the suppression of heresy depended for utility upon its *completeness*.

Let the Cardinal (in reconstructing the Duchy) when the Archbishop and clergy come before him impress on them the importance of especially consecrating to their flocks, and making absolutely vital, such portions of faith and ceremony, however seemingly trivial, as make the approval of the Church a necessity to the life or death of every man however humble. Show that these things are more important to the welfare of the flocks than larger matters, because the means whereby the Church controls the powers of the world to the benefit of souls.

Point out that kings are powerful but by *peoples* and that it is there they must be counterworked.

MEMORANDA ON 'AFFAIRS.' (FOR THE CARDINAL WHEN REORGANIZING THE DUCHY.)

Military. Two great objects with the soldier—to make him feel himself a *part* in such manner as shall not lower individual character. Uniforms appeal to the eye on both these heads. He must *see* the great *One*. He must *see* he is not a murderer.

To check the power of the Barons a standing army must be created out of the lowest ranks.

To make such men soldiers, and to use them afterwards as such, enact the principles of Hannibal's speech to his army in Livy Book xxi.

Flag. The sign of the second great Commandment. The algebra of all that is dearest in and out of oneself.

The less selfish the patriot the more sacred to him the flag, as the symbol of the rights of others.

The new means of destruction which, the Cardinal foresees, are coming into use require new military principles to meet them.

The soldier has to unlearn and learn.

As man he is accustomed to act as a whole and with a view to means *and* ends.

As soldier he must act as part and with view only to means. He has been a being ;—he must learn to be a *function.* The army is the Man ; each man in it is a vital integer of that organic cosmos of nerves, fibres, and atomic matter. The secret is for each integer to be no more and no less in the moment of action ; and to preserve not only his active but his *organic* integrity.

Diplomatic. Fallacy of the axiom concerning firing one's own house.

If the state be an analogue of individual man, the constitution is an analogue of the human constitution for which the individual is not answerable.

The first duty of the Diplomate is to remember that he is a servant and has not to teach the truth but to secure a given result in a given Mind.

The first necessity of the Diplomate is to win the confidence of him he would influence. This to be done by *being* what men can trust: (as distinct from ordinary diplomatic policy which, though more successful in a given case, never can permanently succeed).

This confidence gained the various opinions to be controverted are to be operated on scientifically.

In argument to remember that *the error* is to be conquered, not the errator. The mind in which it has encamped is to be treated not as an enemy's army, but as a country in possession of an invader. The invader is to be expelled not the people. In this expulsion the first step is to raise the populace. By patient dissemination of various incentives, ideas, and other leavening matter, let spontaneous insurrection dispossess the invader of the chief cities and strongholds and force him into the field.

Then comes the attack of direct argument.

Let the Cardinal speak of that beautiful Heaven below which the Catholic Church created, when on the one beautiful day of rest and peaceful equality, in a beautiful edifice, in a Divine palace of visible, and amid beautiful sounds of audible, music, the most beautiful ideas and feelings were communicated to the most beautiful powers of the human mind, by a priesthood consecrated in the Beauty of Holiness.

E.G. Tintern—dedicated to the Virgin.

Cardinal: How like the sure and solemn processes of Nature is that beautiful evolution by which the ceorle and soldier produced the *baro minor*, the *barones minores* the great Lords, and those worldly chieftains excerned those holy Sanctuaries where spotless hands and sainted souls did the work and lived the life of Chastity, Devotion, and Peace.

FOR USE IN MOUTH OF CARDINAL.[1]

I see in the universe evidences of a superhuman wisdom rather than of a Divine. Adaptations of means to ends exquisite and wonderful indeed, but not infallible and sometimes appearing to contravene themselves. A plan of government incalculably beyond human

[[1] Compare a similar idea in Mr. Mill's 'Essays on Nature and Theism.'—J. N.]

amplitude in unity and omnipresence but curiously liable to derangement either *sponte sua* ? or by such small causes as, *e.g.* the 'free-will' of man.

Cardinal to Secretary, (observing the various professions of men around).

How these exist for the true man who is somewhat but not totally each. Somewhat but not totally a soldier, &c. &c.

Yet it is necessary that ordinary men should thus incarnate vocations : for so the results of those vocations can alone be carried through.

The 'true man' is too rare to work, invent, discover in them all. But they, working for him, prepare for him the best fruits of each, to be in him combined.

FROM CARDINAL'S INVOCATION TO HIS LOST EARLY LOVE (HERETICA).

Farewell, till I may see thee once again,
In the clear overhead of my distress
And pitiless perdition, sweet in Heaven,
Like some bright constellation, nor even curse
The clouds that shut thee out, for joy that thou,
Unseen, canst smile no less.

THE CARDINAL (IN THE HEIGHT OF HIS FIRST POPULARITY).

      Day by day
Round my vexed feet the rushing people swirl
And flap my tired eyes with the ragged foam
Of capp'ed welcome. Day by day
I breathe a hotter and a thicker air
Foul with the tenth ten-thousandth reeking mould
Of leaky approbation; night by night
My presence-chamber, like the sky to him
That climbs an Alp, doth flower a lordlier field
Of golden circlets, and the dust of my floors
Is farms and shires broken from jewelled knees
Unused to kneel.
     I act, men say 'well done.'
I speak, and as the famished that draws in
The life draught, silent while his sucking heart
Drains the dry cup and, saved, a moment stands
Still, in a pause of utterless content,
Then leaps in gratulation, so between
My speech and the applause of Kings invenes
The thirsty silence and the full.

HERETICA.

HERETICA SEEING THE CARDINAL.

She read his face as 'twere a sacred book,
And as in such a book we find a text
That tells against us . . . . . .
. . . . till as flash from cloud
The fiery sense flames through the burning word,
The woman that she was in her full flower
Of mortal glory knew his fatal heart
And withered into nothing—

ON FORBIDDING OF SCRIPTURES TO LAITY, CON.

Heretica: The Church does ill to deny the Bible to the People since It is so Divinely Written that every order of mind, and every affection of individual mind, assimilates therefrom that which is specific to it.

The Cardinal answers that the Church as depository of the Holy Spirit is the means by which that specific is eliminated and applied. Heretica replies by speaking of the profundity of the human heart, and by an impassioned interrogative argument founded thereon.

Heretica: We say that the human quality which you, the Church, assume to represent is too Divine to be enacted by anything having the obstructions of a mortal body. That, whereas, It should be the summit of us, you, setting up yourselves to be the top of things, degrade us subordinates by the whole measure of your own inferiority.

(Let Heretica describe the soul and the highest faculty of the soul, and show how under that rare heaven of air the lower qualities expand and expire: *et per contra*.)

Let her, also, show the analogy of the effects of a human priesthood on the general soul with those of a pagan mythology—a deification of *men*.

Heretica: You, the hierarchy, being uninspired, must restrain and deform the growth of this still-young Being— Man. The completeness of your system is the reason for our war with it to the knife. It is a shirt of mail, the size of the boy, in which you shut up the growing creature. The exuberant life within has forced out at every cranny into monstrosities. (Describe the various other effects on the incarcerated body.) We, therefore, fight for life. Better be naked than in such raiment.

Heretica: We—the People—want this printing to give us cheap knowledge, want this knowledge to give us that power over matter which may stand in place of riches and leisure. Want this freedom as the means to that knowledge, &c. &c.

Therefore, our interest and yours are essentially and throughout irreconcilable.

In the judgment scene Heretica must develop and illustrate, by description and *prediction*, the advantages and results of Human Government by Many—in opposition to the Cardinal's demonstration of the contrary—foreshowing how all that *we* now most prize (*e.g.* self-government of every kind) depends on the democratic interpretation of a Church.

'THE PHILOSOPHER.'

[Miscellaneous notes and memoranda concerning 'the Philosopher,' and the theories to be developed by him.]

The Philosopher's room and Pictures.

Pictures, &c. so arranged that things (in different departments of Art) that are closely analogous to each other are associated.

Picture of the human soul—a crowd about a chief. Of the crowd none wholly human—each an embodiment of some functional humanity, or *quasi*-brutality.

The chief alone human—but potentially rather than actively—and with a co-morphology with all the crowd *plus* something else.

Picture of temptation. Some of the crowd endeavouring to move by force, while others unsettle by argument that pale proud 'Chief.'

Picture of knowledge. A human being asleep:

myriads of strange shapes touching, biting, kissing, blowing, whipping, whispering about him.

INVISIBLE FORCES OF THE UNIVERSE.

Let the Philosopher illustrate by scholastic theory of 'intellectus agens et patiens species impressa et expressa,' &c. his notion that the human body itself is a federal unity of *living* constituents : thence let him branch to the outer world and describe the picture he would draw, if he were a painter, wherein the substance of nature should be made up of inextricably intertwined human and other forms, with limbs and features—especially eyes —interlaced, knotted and strained in infinite implication.

Let him also point out that the great Man the Race is federal, and infer thence in confirmation of his theory concerning the individual : again illustrating the Race by that theory.

For Philosopher.

Of my artist-friends one paints a Landscape, and then disentangles from the duller dusker colours of it the living essences which were their life, and makes them blossom into the colours of figures and vestments : another takes the skirt of his heroine and expands it into a Landscape. One floats his figures *in* dusky air, like fish in black water—the water more or less drowning the fish in proportion to its depth; another floats them *en* the yielding water—which cuts a round floating body—so that a man's face stands out one-third *beyond* the canvas. Again another mixes his shadow with his paints so that they seem dulled with dirty oil or water and every colour dirtied *in se*, instead of dimmed by immersion.

RE GIFTS (IN BANQUET-SCENE).

A gift expresses the donor and his idea of the donee. It is sometimes easier to make a binary than a single gift, because the two may modify and explain each other: *e.g.* supposing a quality in one, good in itself, but liable to be liked by common culture for second-rate reasons, you may fix your interpretation of it by something in the other demonstrative of your order of mind. And each may be so complementary and supplementary to the other as to produce a married perfection.

Exempla. White elephant complimentary as implying wealth in donee.

Cameleon—'feeding on air'—(costing nothing)—would be indelicate if this subtle immateriality did not seem so necessary to those interesting peculiarities which make it curious and desirable. Being so, and, therefore, not to be misunderstood, this costlessness becomes a delicacy.

Philosopher in trial scene—re ' Statuæ nuda.'

The Cardinal has laid down the principles of relative (not absolute) indecorum—thus—'impudicitia' in the body is unnecessarily to uncover those portions of it whereof the mere act of uncovering produces, either in the uncoverer or the uncovered, a form or phase of those sensations which would result from utter divestment; mental *impudicitia* is the analogue of the physical; and immodesty, physical or mental, while the same everywhere in principle, differs in practice with individuals, nations, eras, &c.

It may be immodest in a Nun to show her eyes, and he who makes her do so is therefore immodest. It may be immodest in a recluse to let a stranger look him in the face. So of mental Nuns and Hermits.

An Abyssinian woman is not immodest in her exposure: an Abyssinian man might say to her many things intolerable to a European woman or from a European man. So *of* and *from* mental Abyssinians. (Develop these main principles to their details.)

That the Sculptor has exhibited his Venus is not *per*

se criminal, the question for the Court is whether criminal in such and such a community.

The Cardinal in gentle and considerate language, calls on the Sculptor for his defence, from his point of view.

The Sculptor, saying that he speaks with his hands not with his tongue, asks to be allowed to answer by his friend the Philosopher.

Philosopher then, admitting the justice of the Cardinal's principles and their application to tinted statues and the various forms of imitation, defends his friend by reference to the Ideal as distinct from the imperfect. Shows the mental effect of all Perfection and the impossibility that except through Art it can be known to the Multitude or that, as regards human Nature, it can be expressed by art except in the whole human body.

Speculation of Philosopher.

The shore that changes not must be more powerful than the changing sea that cannot change it. Yet we call the sea active and the shore passive. So, in the universe, life, motion that produces change, may be less alive than the motionless and unchanging—nay may be an evidence of diminishing vitality—of being less than Divinely alive. So that all 'living' things are mortal and Death the re-absorption into the motionless of Divine Life.

For Philosopher. 'The Poor and Ignorant.' For him in his normal conditions (of struggle, difficulty, labour, subjection) all sympathy and every helping hand and illuminating effort. For him a 'sovereign' *unit*, a dominating insubordinate individuality, a sledge-hammer on his head and, during due season, hard labour and cat when he comes to: collectively grape-shot followed by the strong government of a many-classed society. For thus only will he be in the condition wherein his best faculties may have healthy exercise—*i.e.* exercise in due relation to his worse.

THE OCCULTATION OF THE PHILOSOPHER'S STAR BY THE MOON.

As the hour advances to the minute all mental obscuration—commencing with the lighter shades of doubt and difficulty—slowly thickens to an agony of blackness coinciding with the moment of mid-occultation; whence a slow return to light by subtle gradations till, as the edge of the star reappears, mental illumination commences, with music of spheres and chorus of angels, and so dawns into the glory of Morning.

Philosopher. But it may be answered [1] that an infallible Church can best dictate to each man and nation the precise application of principle appropriate to him and them.

No: for the application to be virtue must be in the belief that it is the *best possible.* And Divine Infallibility cannot set forth two bests. Therefore Revelation delivers principles absolutely true and leaves imperfect man to apply them.

THE HUMANITY IN BRUTES.

Philosopher. If the human soul is *per se* an evidence of immortality then also is my dog immortal. (Describe the humanity perceived by intimate acquaintance with the Brute. And perceived, also—as in the joy of the Lamb, &c. &c.—by the keen eye without intimate acquaintance.)

My hound lies on the wolf-skin and I doze on the chair. Suddenly we hear, afar-off, the cries of unseen Hunting—and the horn

> That stirs delicious madness. In a moment,
> Like as two dogs, I see the huntsman's passion
> Within me and without : the sight within

[[1] Answered to the saying of the Cardinal that 'Truths are usually accepted by Mankind for the wrong reasons?'—ED.]

Has scarce beheld it when the sense without
Sees, hears, and feels it from the empty wolf-skin
Rush to the door, in nose, eyes, mouth and ears
That shape it, with four legs to bear it up
From the drawing earth and push it to its will,
And so much body as may blood the whole
And engine it and skurry it on the prey.
Likeness? if this is likeness and no more
Or less than kind for kind, then farewell faith
That makes us men with men, for, by my soul,
The eyes that we call human, and wherein,
Since men began, who calls himself a man
Says in his heart that he beholds mankind,
Are not so merely me.

For Philosopher or Cardinal on Truth.

(In illustration of sub-truths and untruths in the machinery of the spiritual and Social World.)

See the physical world : see the *ambush* of the *carnivora*—*i.e.* the practical assertion of their *absence* to the victim. But you answer—'these things are the work of *quasi*-humanity in them. They are actions of beings who *might* act otherwise.' See the ant-lion in his pit, with the circumvallation of *moveable* sand, and himself expectant at the unseen bottom: or the spider's treacherous mathematics. You say 'these works may be the unconscious result of dispositions to move and act in certain directions, and the baneful agency of them an accident of their necessary properties.' But what do you say to the Chameleon turning in the sun, in which he delights with the delighting butterfly, into what that butterfly must mistake for a patch of green and yellow flowers, and, so mistaking, come within range of that spring-jack hand that will transfer it to a moth-hawk 'gape.' In this case the bait is not an action commonly so called, but a physiological change, occurring in the sun whether with or without butterflies.

NOTES AND MEMORANDA CONCERNING 'THE PHILOSOPHER'S' LECTURES.

The Cardinal, wishing to spare the Philosopher, and to conciliate the rising Learning, in order to turn rather than to destroy it, orders that—as the Philosopher is charged with heresies—he shall give his usual course of Lectures, and clerical deputies, appointed by the Cardinal, shall attend and report on them. The Cardinal himself hearing that which is given at the mass-hour on the trial-day.

The Philosopher has a struggle, whether to temporize,

by suppressing what he would otherwise have said in these Lectures, or to speak as usual. His interview with Heretica confirms him in his resolution to be merely true—neither ostentatious nor negative.

The Philosopher lectures on the Ideal, and, under guise of sermon *Ecce Homo*, condensing his whole system of ideals, moral and intellectual, exposes thence a theory of virtue, individual and national, essentially antagonistic to despotic human authority, political or spiritual.

In this lecture let the Philosopher say—'We want a Man—Christ should not be in the Heavens but on Earth.'

Let him allude to Sebonde—(for extract from whom see Historical Note-book.) [1] Let him also allude to the Cardinal's description of an ideal world, which some of his audience had heard, and show that it is deficient because *minus* that Man. In it let him *per contra*, allude to the rule of the multitude as newly proposed in certain meetings known to some of his audience and show that it is equally deficient and for what reasons.

[1] Extract from Sebonde, professor of Medicine at Barcelona before 1440:—

'Quam quidem sapientiam—(*i.e.* "sapientiam in creaturis scriptam") nullus potest videre, neque legere per se in dicto libro semper aperto (*i.e.* Nature) nisi fuerit a Deo illuminatus et a peccato originali mundatus.' Till then he is merely 'aptus ad suscipiendum eam,' but 'nullam doctrinam neque sapientiam habeat actu.'

NOTES FOR PHILOSOPHER'S LECTURES ON THE IDEAL AND THE ARTS AND SCIENCES.

We, men, enquire the Philosophy of Man. The standard of each Being in Nature is its ideal specimen. Of Man, therefore, the Ideal Man.

He has the power to express and this power being perfect he does whatever precisely transfers the *transferenda*. This transference is action. The perfect soul acts through the perfect body. The body is ruled by a heart beating exact intervals. Perfect bodily action must be in times-bearing proportion to that central beat —*i.e.* rhythmical. His actions, therefore, are rhythmical. Rhythm is order in motion.

We see the perfect Man with Perfect Men. They are equal by Nature, but, since no two can stand on the same spot of the veritable earth, their *circumstances* differ (age, place, accident, &c.)—and there is not equality.

As all are good there can be no feeling but Love : as all are spontaneous there will be freedom. Liberty, Order (since not equal), Fraternity, are therefore, the principles of their social union.

The ideal Man being as aforesaid we have to view

the imperfect in relation to him. Those relations are of two kinds.

I. The imperfect temporarily, and in special functions, rises to (or near to) identity with the perfect. His spontaneities herein are the Arts.

II. The imperfect supplements his imperfection by *Laws* : hence morals, politics, rhetoric—(the persuasion of imperfects) &c.

(*Memorandum*. The Greeks called all the fine Arts Music, and threw the problem a grade further back by saying that their cause was the Muses—nine beautiful humanities.)

No Arts but Nature and that Nature Man—who if he were perfect would need no arts, but, being imperfect, needs a thousand arts to compass the one Nature.

The perfect human Being is and does. The Arts are of Being—and of Doing—other Arts are subdivisions of these.

1. The Art of Being—is Love, with such functions as are necessary to it. Love, the passion toward unity, would cease in unity, and implies, therefore, individuality.

2. The Art of Doing has three subarts,—the art of knowing, the art of feeling, and the art of saying. All other Arts of action are sub-divisions of these.

To do is to move. To move from within towards without is 'to feel.' To move from without towards within is 'to know.' To move so, or so far, as to cause motion in others is 'to say.'

To will? To will is to feel the movement of whatever function is concerned therein. (Throughout this investigation we do not ask the what but the *how*.) To will, therefore, is a species of 'to feel.'

Memorandum. To begin the demonstration by showing the Art of doing, with its subarts, in their ideal specimens, (taking 'knowing and saying' and thence inferring 'feeling') and from thence deduce the art of Being.

Then to show Christianity's Love to be them all; inasmuch as Love is both Being and Doing. Thence infer that He who both *lived* and preached Love was the Ideal which has been shown to be the living *Ratio quid* of all Law—the Perfect who needs no 'arts.'

FOR LECTURE ON CIVILIZATION.

Civilization is the process of development in Mankind.

To develop is to *un*hide: *un*hide what? Not substance existing in the person or thing developed, for in the best known developments the matter is derived *ab extra*. To unhide, therefore, an immaterial somewhat—to realize a Law of change—'*Legem naturare*'—that is to show both the order and appearance of those 'necessary' varieties which a Unity exhibits in attaining its ideal state.

Development, therefore, is a process of Creation, whether in what we call an embryonic, or in that post-'Embryonic,' creature which is no less an embryon.

Growth is a change in bulk not *idea*.

To place things so that the Many become One is to construct.

To place things so that the One become Many is to destroy.

But a higher order may displace to better-place, and temporary destruction may be a phase of construction. The higher the order the more temporary the destruction. The displacement and replacement is organic and is called development.

FOR LECTURE ON THEOLOGY.

Truth is things as perceived by the Perfect Man. But we have seen that he himself is the One Standard of all human things.

How then, as truth is things as perceived by Him, can we, who are imperfect, have the truth concerning Himself?

Only through His own utterance : *i.e.* Revelation.

But why, on this head as on others, is not the temporarily transfigured Man (*i.e.* genius) sufficient? Because in the welfare of the soul we must have not approximate truth, as in Art, but truth (humanly) absolute.

Faith. Since Truth is that which the ideal Man would spontaneously receive, Religious Truth is incongruous with the imperfect man and incomprehensible. It is necessary, therefore, that there must be in the Christian who would receive Religious Truth a reconstruction of the moral and spiritual functions—a transfiguration towards the Ideal Man. This, and the power to undergo this, is πίστις—the Platonic word being borrowed by the Apostle as the most consistent term for a fact new to Paganism.

TO BE DEVELOPED BY PHILOSOPHER.

In the high type and lower types of conscience we have Christ, and the Kings, Priests, and Judges of Judaism.

The first, in itself a revelation, testifying in the midst

of the other mental functions, suggesting heights of impossible virtue, finally rejected of them, crucified, suffering a temporary abeyance, and rising shortly to a Heaven of ἔκστασις, whence it returns to judge the quick and dead actions of the rest and, at last, to rule in the congruity of Millenium.

The other types, blindly and partially, by Urim and Thummim, and other mediations gaining occasional Messages from Heaven.

But because of these invisible Christs and Prophets are the visible mythic? When I was on the north coast a whale was cast ashore, and on cleaving its paddle of blubber I found the human hand inside.

But because of that invisible hand has my visible hand become mythical?

It is in the nature of the truest facts, as facts, that they exist in two or three regions of realization *at once*, and the existence in an invisible form is in itself an argument not against but *for* the existence elsewhere in a visible.

If all the hungry were fed, the naked clothed, the weeping comforted, how much time would remain for Science and Philosophy?

But how if by Science I ensure food and clothing to thousands unborn?

How if by Philosophy I raise the souls of generations of men to higher charities and, by their hands, am truly almsgiving to nations of men?

But how if *not*?

Yet if a man till a field that shall support a parish, and spend all his life and substance in the tillage, and die ere harvest, and the enemy destroy his work, has he not his reward?

And shall not I also?

In the will and motive the deed is done already.

But who shall certify of my will and motive?

THE CHANCELLOR.

The Chancellor and Baron in consultation [after the arrival of the Cardinal to reorganize the Duchy].

Baron says that the Chancellor must act swiftly and strongly—being in such peril.

Chancellor replies—No—that for the present all he must do is to gain Time. All violent action—when the end is not immediate—is dangerous, because it produces reaction: Wisdom is to wait upon Nature and push her just beyond her intention. Schemes that extend through Time should never be positive, but negative, since the chain may be broken by one of the Unforeseeables and Inevitables, and the cause and effect be thus killed.

Maintain your inch of *terra-firma* footing, and wait the opportunity.

Spend your time in waiting, but not in action. Let the flower grow a year and blossom in a day. The wise man attends upon the forces of Nature.

There are always imprisoned Spirits who can do all but let themselves free. The wise man frees them. He pushes the tottering stone from the wall. Cuts the string of the hanging fruit. Slips the chained dog. Drives the prey into the Lion's sight. Waits till the Falcon is hungry.

Nature, like the teeming Elephant, has her moments of parturient weakness: watch for them and strike her into meat, or bind her into service.

Never meet a wave at its flow—wait the reflux, follow it and push it home. Prune a plant vigorously once a year, it flourishes: hack it a little daily, it withers. Plunge your enemy in water he glows to new strength; keep him damp, at half the expenditure of moisture, and you soak out his rheum-sodden life. Nurse the purpose of your enemy and overlay it.

In wrestling be the willow—wouldst thou throw back the ball of thy foe's strength? But if violence be needful, let him sharpen the knife for thee, which wrest at the last moment, and stab.

Men walk by nature differently—some erect in the sun; others, like the toad, creep from shadow to shadow.

Never allow your enemy an advantage, however small, it may be the *terra-firma* of a more important success.

Never wound a friend without killing him.

Trust not a dead snake till he stinks. Never forsake a living friend, for while there is life there is hope: he may be again powerful, and you, then, lose not only him but your character.

Chaplain: What a joke to think 'of one blood all nations of men!' Thou and I for instance, and this fool (the Cardinal) who sends me thus to thee whom he would destroy!

Chancellor: Do not brag out of thy belief. Man is man: thou thyself, if thou lookest well into it, hast known moments when thou wouldest have been almost as foolish.

Chancellor: Do away Religion? Will you do away with the human stomach—put down hunger? No, we will respect Bread while it is the necessity of Human Nature. You and I may know it is but dung and dust—the more likely that Dust should cry out for it! but it is only while the dung and dust are not perceptible that they can be food of Man. Bah, Boy, take thy bread. Eat *if* thou canst: sell *for* thou canst. Shall thy neighbour starve because thou art nice? Nay why not take thy mess with the savoury difference? God save thee from the gnawing of an empty belly—ay, though thou make Him to the purpose; and if the wafer be matter or spirit—dirt or the flower of dirt—who cares? Thou art filled and canst rot more passably.

CHANCELLOR AND CHAPLAIN.

Chaplain: Shall I give A so and so?

Chancellor: No need to play so high. He covets Z's barony. Moreover Y's brother shamed him before the Court at ———. Give him ———

Chaplain: But why give at all?—his grudges are enough.

Chancellor: He hath a conscience, boy. Give him ———. 'Tis a trifle, but he will work like Apollyon and call it all gratitude. Pay B so heavily that he shall feel if I fall the gift will be resumed as self-shown corruption. But make it not as a gift or he will hate me for the obligation. Concede it as an old right recognized. D hath in these six months had his honour kicked at from every Court in Europe. Write and say I trust implicitly to his honour. Yet—lest he feel it a jest—say thy master grieveth that it is now two years since he hath heard mention of his name. What a thing is Man! I know he loveth not me nor my cause, yet shall he give his life for this breath—foul breath.

———

In indicating (to the Chaplain) the hidden motives of the *haute noblesse*, among those to whom he writes, let the Chancellor point out the connection between Kingship and the democratically-supplied Priesthood as his support against the Nobles and the consequent vital jealousy of the Nobles of the power of the Church. Also the jealousy of the higher and monastic—and therefore powerful priesthood—as compared with the lower clergy.

Chancellor to Chaplain: As sound out of a bell, as pleasure in flesh, as insects in water, as mould upon all, so God is a perturbation and ferment of the Soul. How then create the Worlds? Bah, nothing is but thinking, and that thought which is the necessary First creates the cogitated Universe. Set Him at nought? By no means. That single hair of one water-atom is not mould : that unmet movement of one bell-atom is not sound.

The ideas Man discourses of and worships are the creatures of his various faculties. Therefore turn from the ideas to the faculties. The ideas are useful in their effect on them, but he is a bungling workman who acts by such reflexes. The true artist finds directer means.

This Me stands firm . . . .
. . . . while faculties and passions,
Kneaded and modelled to a kind of man,
Like a tame monkey, antic in my tether
And ape the tricksey round of human change,
But at the check-string leap back to their place
Upon the master's poll.

THE ABBOT, BROTHER TO THE POPE.

[The following passages are, it will be seen, a parody on the super-subtleties of mediæval monkish pedantry and fanaticism, and an indication of the phrenzy in which they frequently culminated.— ED.]

The Abbot: The world will be dissolved into the invisible. We shall not see nor feel it; yet we shall see and feel. Therefore we shall see or feel as in a dream. Dreamlife is the true life, therefore, and to be cultivated by all who would prefer the permanent to the temporary.

The Abbot to his Chaplain: Hearing is saying inverted. The mouth of the soul that emits each word with its special shapes, receives with the same gesture. Thy words are noise till I hand them into me as I should hand them out if I spake. How am I the better then for thy reading? Nay, far worse. For the soul's mouth in an ecstasy of action endeavours to adjust itself to thy rapid utterance till the very strings of life are tangled and split; and if it be ill to hand out my words indecorously, when, being out, they are no longer receiving my ill-usage, how much worse to hand them in amiss, when every thought I think is more inextricably complicating the blasphemy.

The Chaplain promises to think over this difficulty

and at the next interview suggests. *Chaplain:* Thou art wise and knowest, I am ignorant. Command me to read to thee decorously. Thou art now free from my disobedience. I, 'knowing not,' shall be beaten with few stripes—*i.e.* it is a light offence. Thou, therefore, considering my occupations in the Church's affairs, do penance for me daily.

[The Abbot is pleased: the experiment is tried: when it ceases to satisfy, the Chaplain again suggests.]

Chaplain: Aristotle saith a thing consists of beginning, middle and end. Therefore the whole possible expression of any word hath these. Now let the beginning be Divine—as indeed agreeth with that text '*in Principio*'—the middle half Divine half human—the end human. Pronounce each word three times, appropriately, and as thou hast completed all expression thou must have included every part of expression.

The Abbot is delighted, but soon again in despair. For as three things cannot be said at once, and the right expression is not given till the three are said, in what case is he *between* the sayings, while the word is said and not rightly? Idolatry. Blasphemy. Hell.

The Chaplain again suggests.

Chaplain: These words are not yours but his who wrote them to you—they are what he intended them, not what they would otherwise mean.

The Abbot: Worse and worse, for they are the Infallible Pope's and infallible. I—fallible—*cannot*, therefore mean the exact same. Wretched me!

Chaplain: But the Pope is your brother—he commences 'dear Brother.' Brother is convertible. (Brethren are equal; if he to you, you to him.) Therefore if you are fallible, as you feel, the Pope indicates that herein he speaks but as fallible man.

Abbot: But still the uncertainty remains as to his precise meaning.

Chaplain: Which we will remedy thus. I write his Holiness that you are too ill to read and crave him to address his sacred epistle to *me*. Now in writing to me he will write as infallible. I, fallible, *cannot* mean his meaning. Consequently there is no sin in my misreading. I then affix my misreading to each word—by respective signs—and you shall read without difficulty that to which I have affixed mine own significance, and which can mean nor more nor less than I mean by it.

Abbot in infinite delight and relief.

On the same principle of reasoning the Chaplain gets the Abbot to sign a number of blank parchments in order that he may fill them up. By this means he is able to write as he will to the Pope with the appearance of the Abbot's authority.

DEATH OF THE ABBOT.

I know you very well—you are Apollyon.
If you were not the wickedest Saint in Heaven
You well might be the ugliest.
                    This is hell then.
'And He descended into hell'

Which is the 'third day'? Call me on the third day:
Do you hear ——?—I am a strong sleeper,—
Call me on the third day. As it began to dawn—
Ay, or a little earlier—for the journey—
The heart of the earth—
At present good night. Yes; yes;
Not so loud, not so loud. Who's there, who are you?
I know your beak, friend, we have met before—
Let me see, let me see,—somewhere in Egypt—
You went to the wall—the weakest goes to the wall—
What, we have tussled then? What, we have fought?
I put you to the wall—you and your crew—
Flat as nailed kites squabbed by a thousand winters—
You and your crew, you and your paunchless crew,
The cat-head and the fish-head and the dog-head—
Why here they are—I know you gentlemen—
Good-morrow, Baal, Bual, Beelzebub, Pol, Phoibus,
Lucifer—slip your names, you can't run justice—

Good morrow, Belial—Master Molock God,
Give you good-day—you need it by your looks.—
Oh ah! I see you are the spirits in prison,
Well you are white enough—You shake, sirs—what?
You have heard something lately? *Predicavit* —
That's it? Yes, yes this was no friar-preacher,
No louse-pate tickle-ear,—no, no mar text—
Credunt Diaboli—I give you joy,
I wouldn't believe so if I were all nails
And burnt as ill as leather—
                        I know your pitchfork, too,
Up there the sweet Provençal muck-masters
Are clawed in such a fashion. You smell like them—
Go to your gongs. Faugh, you are nasty beauties
You dung your roses here. Ay, make hay, make hay;
'Tis hot enough.

    The Abbot, at his dying moments—being alone—awakes to the remembrance of the youth that preceded the long arid desert of life.

    The clearing shapes are as forms out of a snowstorm, or out of smoke as it clears. The strain of the mind to grasp them.

    The sense of distance, yet of decreasing distance—of two entities (the present and the past) that will be one, as when by cross of eye two images of the same thing are seen that come together, each on each, in one, not of combination but of identity.

They come so near that only a diaphanous pane seems to divide them, as the clear wall of a new honey-comb divides honey from honey.

Another strain—something gives way—they are passing through this wall as honey to honey. They move more swiftly, as a dislocated bone that under the strain of the surgeon nears the socket.

He forefeels the shock of re-union—another moment—another moment—ah this deadly faintness ! they will be one—they are.

>Oh thou that lookedst on me in those days
>Look on me now .   .   .   .   .   .
> .   .   .   .   lest I die.
>My soul is sickened with a wild desire—
>Thou *shalt* look on me !
>I see thee—as in a haze—
>I strain as to move the world—
>All the weight of all matter seems upon me—but I move it, I move it !
>Thou art nearer—nearer—I see   .   .   .
>Thou livest—I live—
>Ah my heart—(*dies.*)

MISCELLANEOUS MEMORANDA FOR THE DRAMA.

As the Evening Star, broadening its petals like a flower and exhaling beyond the luminous visible a fragrance of unseen light, if a cloud sail below it, without any crest of mist that the eye can see, brails [1] its radiance and draws in its rays till but a central disc remains, and thus by its more delicate essence shows the impurity our senses cannot perceive, so her shrinking nature closed upon itself in presence of, to us, invisible unbeauty.

In a vision of Heaven. Let the process of the season from earliest spring to midsummer be the analogue to furnish *principles* for the description. Then at culmination, when language has reached its utmost, let the visionary be conscious of a sudden entry into

[1] Brails, the small sails of a ship: to brail, to haul up, or draw in, such small sails.—ED.]

something beyond, of which however, as an organ changes its stops, he has no remembrance on returning to the point of departure.

Draw the Daimons of Creation. Each not charged with a particular Kingdom of Nature but a special *function*: taking the human body as the type and ruling the analogous provinces throughout Nature: *e.g.* the manual δαίμων &c. Each attended by their subordinates.

Anacreon—'Ἐπὶ μυρσίναις τερείναις—says 'why dost thou anoint a stone, and pour gifts on the ground? Cease from vain oblation—rather anoint me while I live.' Show that he was less wise than the blind Idolator.

For a Heresy.[1] All Mankind is the Word of God— the third person in the Trinity. What else in the universe *speaks*?

Found an argument (*per colloquium?*) on 'present

[1] See Hegel, &c.—J. N.]

your bodies a *living* sacrifice.' *Sacer* carries no necessary idea of pain, death, or denial.

A CONDEMNED.

And these are so heedless of my dear flesh, so hard to me, as if I were wood or stone and had not these exquisite nerves, these all-admirable conformations! These that once were so otherwise, so attendant on my steps, so preventive of my every wish! And yet then in those days they seemed not to me one whit too gentle nor to have a grace or sweetness more than was native and necessary to me.

DEMOS.

Depict a meeting of young enthusiasts in newly liberated Thought setting forth their nascent *systems* on every subject.

Proposed. A sitting of the Collegiate 'Demos.'

A picture of all the wild extravagancies of new-born discovery, ambition, and speculation.

HYPOTHESES ON THEOLOGY (FOR DEMOS).

Is God, then, an Idea only, the abstraction and synopsis of the principles of the Universe made by the unifying human mind and possessing therefore all the attributes of an idea—' Whom no man hath seen at any time '—' A Spirit '—' Dwelling not in Temples made with hands ? '

It is not true to say that the Universe is God, because the Universe which we perceive is only the effect on our perceptions of the Action of Somewhat we cannot perceive.

The sensible universe is therefore ourselves. It is true, therefore, to say God creates the universe, and creates it out of nothing, in the sense in which our sensation of a blow is corporeally nothing.

To say the Universe is God is not to say that God is subject to change, inasmuch as the essential Universe may be unchangeable though producing changing sensations in us ; as God produces various emotions in our souls.

The Universe of Matter is in a state, as it were, of fermentation, whereby some portions thereof attain to a subtler condition of greater mobility, which manifests more apparently and readily the principles which in duller fashions, through due degrees, the rest observes. These subtler portions are spirit.

Suppose the Universe to be an assemblage of living souls of limited cognition, each able to perceive certain others only, and knowing and performing its Duties towards these?

Is God the Universal Doer, but has Man, nevertheless, a privilege of *choice* as to the action to take place?

' How came you by this Christianity? By vision, by ecstasy?'

Balder: ' Much more calmly and surely. I was in the very dust. I had found—I will say how another time—the impotence of Philosophy. I had trusted to the heart and found myself in the act of murder. I found my whole soul crying out for a revelation of Truth, and I began to think that what was a necessity of Nature must exist somewhere. The thirsty eye sees water. The starving man beholds visible bread, by the instinct of the body for its want.'

When it was known that the Almighty Lord who once did walk in Jewry had returned to this world and had His Throne in the City of David, and that all who were weary and heavy laden came unto Him and had rest, then the man who was once called Balder, but now ——, arose with his wife to go unto the Lord that He might heal the scar upon her breast.

www.ingramcontent.com/pod-product-compliance
Lightning Source LLC
Chambersburg PA
CBHW020236240426
43672CB00006B/549